£2.95

KU-793-466

Here 18.

Social Surveys for Social Planners

GODFREY GARDNER

THE OPEN UNIVERSITY PRESS
Milton Keynes

ISBN 0 335 00239 0

The Open University Press
12 Cofferidge Close, Stony Stratford
Milton Keynes, MK11 1BY, England

First published in this edition 1978 by The Open University Press.

Copyright © 1976 Holt-Saunders Pty. Ltd.,
All rights reserved. No part of this work may be reproduced in any form, by mimeograph or
any other means, without permission in writing from the publisher.

Photoset by G.T. Setters Pty. Limited, Sydney.

Printed by South China Photo-Process Printing Co. Ltd., Hong Kong.

Contents

Acknowledgments

The author and publisher have made every effort to trace the ownership of all copyrighted selections found in this book and to make full acknowledgment for their use. If any error has occurred, the publisher expresses sincere regret and will be pleased to make the necessary corrections in future editions.

Grateful acknowledgment is made to the following authors, publishers, agents, corporations, and individuals for their permission to reprint copyrighted materials.

Addison-Wesley Publishing Co. Inc. for the extract 'A Filter Item' by Maccoby and Maccoby from *Handbook of Social Psychology* ed. G. Lindzey;

George Allen & Unwin Ltd for the extract from *An Outline of Philosophy* by Bertrand Russell;

Australian Electoral Office for the actual results of the May 1974 Federal elections;

ANOP for the May 1974 Federal elections poll;

ASRB for the May 1974 Federal elections poll;

Herald and Weekly Times Limited for the May 1974 APOP Federal election poll;   GALLUP

H.M. Stationery Office for the extract from the Skeffington Report, *People and Planning*;

The Roy Morgan Research Centre Pty Ltd for the May 1974 Morgan Gallup (who is the only Australian member of Gallup International) Federal election poll;

National Institute of Industrial Psychology for the extract from 'Notes on Report Writing' by R.B. Buzzard from the *Journal of Occupational Psychology*;

PEP for the extract from the Broadsheet 544 'Racial Disadvantage in Employment' and from *New Society*;

Pergamon Press Ltd for the extract from *Readings in Urban Sociology* by R.E. Pahl; for the extract from *Methods of Social Research* by Margaret Stacey;

Public Opinion Quarterly for the extracts from 'No opinion, Don't know, and Maybe no answer' by Leo Bogart and 'Is survey postcard verification effective?' by M. Hauck;

J.H. Robb for the extract from *Working-class anti-Semite: a psychological study in a London borough*, Tavistock Publications, London, 1954;

Gordon Stanley for the extracts from 'Attitudes to Women Scale' published in *Australian Psychologist*, 1975, 10 (2).

Preface

This book is intended for all those who are interested in understanding how social surveys work. I also had in mind the needs of social science students in universities and colleges of advanced education; at some stage they are usually required to take part in a social survey or at least draft a questionnaire or conduct some interviews. The book will provide useful guidelines for researchers wishing to carry out their own surveys. In addition a much wider range of readers might like to know how to tell a good survey from a bad one.

Social planners are increasingly dependent upon the kind of information provided by social surveys. They often need to carry out a survey or take part in one without having had any training in social survey methods; I hope this book will meet their special interests.

Social surveys have almost become part of our way of life. Hardly a week passes without at least one being mentioned in the newspapers. The range of topics is no longer restricted to election forecasts and public opinion polls on issues of the day; everything comes under scrutiny — our attitudes, beliefs and opinions, our activities, hopes and fears.

The methods used are sometimes more journalistic than scientific, as for example when broadcasters take recording equipment into the street and ask a few people what they think of the latest Government proposal; this is known, I believe, as 'pop vox'. Other surveys use more systematic methods, including pre-tested standardised questions and scientifically selected random samples. Sample surveys may vary in size from less than a hundred to several thousand people, but sometimes a survey includes everyone, as in a population census.

Psychologists and sociologists are still probably the principal users of social surveys. But they have been joined by students and research workers in anthropology, commerce, economics, geography, history, political science, and town-planning, who are also increasingly involved in social planning. This means that the need for accuracy in social surveys is even greater than before. If social planning is based on poor information, the community may suffer. Academics can bury their mistakes in theses or correct them in subsequent work; social planners often do not get a second chance.

This book should help social planners and others to evaluate social survey reports. It should also help them to conduct their own social surveys — or, if they do not have the necessary resources and decide to call in professional help, to appreciate the problems involved and be able to ask relevant questions and make sensible suggestions at all stages.

Though social surveys are now widely accepted and useful we must not assume that everyone understands why they are necessary. The first two chapters attempt to justify the use of social surveys by describing their purposes and the kind of information that they provide. A social survey needs to be planned along the lines suggested in Chapter 3. The survey design and the questions to be asked have to be worked out in advance, and a timetable set out in order to allow adequate time for the various steps involved.

If we wish to investigate human behaviour and personal preferences, we can either watch people or ask them questions. Chapters 4, 5 and 6 describe these basic methods, warts and all, so that any weaknesses or difficulties in the methods can be clearly understood and remedied as far as possible. In Chapter 7 the two main methods of asking questions, namely in person or through a printed form, are compared. On the basis of these chapters it should be possible to choose the most appropriate survey method according to the purpose and circumstances of the survey.

Sampling methods are explained and some procedures outlined in Chapter 8. This is followed in Chapter 9 by a look at some general problems in sampling which may upset the well-designed plan. Guidelines are given in Chapters 10 and 11 on how to handle and report the results.

Finally, the book ends as it begins, by questioning the necessity for social surveys. But whereas the first chapter states quite dogmatically some reasons why surveys might be needed, Chapter 12 raises a few criticisms of social surveys and controversial issues — not with the intention of settling them but in order to show that the debate continues at a different level.

I am aware that I have not been consistent in citing the sources for the evidence in support of many generalisations in this book. In some cases, usually where details have been given, the reference is cited; in others no evidence is mentioned and this is because

(a) though there are many references available I doubt if I could select the one most suitable for this book;

or

(b) the point is usually accepted by experienced survey practitioners (though this does not mean that it is right);

or

(c) there is no evidence that I know of.

Though some of my statements are unsupported I hope that they are not insupportable! Perhaps they may stimulate further research into methods.

This book has grown out of my series of lectures in the Department of Town and Regional Planning and my practical sessions in the Department of Psychology at the University of Melbourne during the past decade. I am grateful for the encouragement that I have received from both Departments. I am especially grateful to my colleagues Warren Bartlett and Peter Burgoyne for their comments on various sections of the draft, and to Irene Kinsman for her valuable assistance in typing with care and intelligence. My appreciation is extended to Joy Boenisch Burrough for her thoughtful editorial assistance and many suggestions for improving the text. Above all, my wife Friedl deserves 'a medal or be even made a knight' or something for her unfailing patience and support; no social scientist could be more unsociable than I have been whilst writing this book.

Godfrey Gardner

Glossary of Terms

attitude
a relatively enduring and consistent set of opinions, often implying a value judgment, about particular persons or objects (p. 13)

attribute
population characteristics such as race, religion (cf. variable)

bias
systematic error (or distortion) in the data; may derive from a variety of sources, e.g. sampling procedures, non-response, question wording, respondent, interviewer

classification data
information about respondents used to identify responses as coming from particular sub-groups in the sample (p. 37)

closed questions
questions that restrict respondents to a limited set of response categories (p. 42)

code
a value category of a variable or attribute; used for purposes of numerical data analysis

coding
the process of translating information on a variable (or attribute) into categories or numerical values suitable for data analysis

confidence level
the degree of certainty with which a statement may be made about a population (p. 125)

control variables
variables (or attributes) used for dividing of the sample into relevant sub-groups; may guide sampling decisions as well as data analysis (p. 93)

correlation coefficient
a descriptive statistic that estimates the strength of a relationship between variables

data
the body of information collected

demographic characteristics
certain characteristics conventionally used to describe populations, e.g. age, sex, social class, etc.

descriptive statistics
statistics that describe the survey population in quantitative terms (cf. inferential statistics) (p. 123)

exploratory work
study of the research population carried out as a preliminary to the survey proper; may be used to explore issues, see the kind of language, concepts, phrases, etc. used by members of that population

hypothesis
1. predictions (from theory) about the direction of relationships between variables
2. more loosely, ideas about the nature of relationships between variables, or even broad expectations of the outcome of the research

inferential statistics
estimates of the characteristics of a population from a sample survey; requires a sample to be selected by random (not judgmental) methods; also used for hypothesis testing (p. 125)

interview
conversation in which a researcher (or his/her deputy) collects information from a respondent; usually face to face

– formal
set form; the same questions in same order for all respondents

– group
interviewer monitored or guided discussion among a group of informants

– informal
no set form, approximating an ordinary conversation

interviewers manual
instruction book for interviewers

interview schedule
document (questionnaire) that an interviewer uses for asking questions; it may also be used by the interviewer for recording the respondent's answers (p. 35)

matched samples
samples of a population having the same demographic and/or other relevant characteristics

open (-ended) questions
questions that permit the respondent to answer in his own way

panel studies	studies that collect data from the same people at two or more points in time; often used for measuring change or trends
parameters	the characteristics (or attributes) of a population
pilot survey	trial run for the main survey; test of the survey design, instruments, procedures, etc.
population	all the people or units under investigation; the collectivity from which the sample is drawn
– survey	the population actually covered, whether in total or by sampling
– target	the population the survey aims to cover
pre-coding	1. determining response categories (codes) in advance of data collection 2. inclusion of coding categories into the questionnaire for completion by the interviewer (or respondent in the case of a self-completion questionnaire)
pre-testing	checking the suitability of the wording of questions and the proposed response categories
probability sampling	the procedure used to obtain a random sample for which the probability (e.g. a one in ten chance) of selection can be specified for each person (or unit) in the population (p. 91)
questionnaire	the document on which the survey questions are set out; sometimes reserved for the documents which respondents fill out themselves (cf. interview schedule)
reliability	the consistency of repeated measurements under comparable conditions
sample	sub-set of a population selected either for convenience (non-random sample) or systematically selected by statistically sound means to be truly representative of that population (random sample)
– non-random	sampling procedures which do not ensure that every person (or unit) has an equal chance of being included; probably biassed, un-representative
– random	each person (or unit) has an equal chance of being selected and the selection is determined entirely by chance (p. 90)
– quota	a sub-set of the population chosen by non-random sampling methods; achieves a research sample which reflects the characteristics of the population in certain respects, but which is not necessarily representative in all respects
– stratified	based on prior division of the population into sub-populations or strata; selection of people or units is done within strata
sampling error	the error attributable to the fact that a sample is being taken, rather than a complete enumeration; with random sampling procedures the error limits can be calculated (p. 11)
significance	a result (or difference) is said to be statistically significant if it could not have occurred by chance more than an acceptable proportion of times (usually five out of a hundred) (p. 126)
standard error	the estimated range of the error that could be due to using a sample rather than the entire population under investigation (p. 111)
statistic	an estimate of a population parameter obtained through a sample
validity	the extent to which a measure is an index of what it purports to measure or describes what the researcher thinks it describes
variable	population characteristics that vary quantitatively among members of the population, e.g. age, income, political attitudes
weighting	a procedure that makes allowances for any unequal proportions in the sampling of sub-categories within the population under investigation

Chapter 1

Why Do a Survey?

This is a reasonable question. In the days before social surveys were popular this question would be asked by the sceptic because he was not convinced that the method could yield any useful information. It might also be asked by the cynic who did not intend to use the information anyway, or who doubted if anyone else would. But today we might ask the same question for different reasons. It does make sense to question whether time and effort, and money, should go into a survey when the information might not help us solve the problem, or might be obtained more economically in some other way, perhaps by asking experts or by consulting records. In general, the purpose of a survey is to provide information. Planning of any sort is based on information; the more accurate and comprehensive the information the better can be the planning. The hopes of the community may then be achieved more fully, so that people enjoy the kind of life they prefer. Our responsibility is to see that we get accurate and appropriate information in the most efficient way.

Planning of any kind ultimately affects people, and their lives may be better or worse as the result. In social planning it is essential to know about these people and to understand some of their problems.

Before providing new or better services for a community, the needs of the people in that community should be found out. Examples of such services might include: pre-natal clinics; child-care centres; schools; recreation and social facilities; health centres and hospitals; and practical assistance for the elderly as well as the more general requirements of shopping facilities and public transport. Making the best use of land, public money, and natural resources requires information about people as well as about physical features and finance. Decisions about where to put new towns, freeways, shops, and local roads are likely to be better decisions if more is known about the kind of people who will be affected or who will live in the area. Commercial organisations find that they need information from social surveys in order to increase their sales and services. Social planners should be wary of relying on intuition alone.

Social surveys can provide information on

(a) the kind of people who live in the community;

(b) what they do for a living, their education, and their houses;

(c) their other activities — e.g. shopping, hobbies, recreation, travelling;

(d) their views on all of this, and on the locality, and on wider issues.

In what way does this differ from the census? The official census is a form of survey that can give us general information about specific geographical areas. For example, the census has figures on such things as the density of population, the average number of people per dwelling, and the average number of children per family. From the census we can also learn something about an area in terms of the age distribution and number of people in each occupational group. In the United Kingdom, and in Australia since 1971, the census includes information on how far people have to travel to work.

Census information often provides the essential general picture; but it might still be necessary to check, by means of a sample, whether there have been any changes since the date of the census. For many purposes the census is not sufficient; it tells us little about what people do (apart from occupation and travelling to work), and nothing about what they think. In other words the census lacks information about people's lives and ideas.

By talking with some of the real people behind the paper statistics we may gain a better understanding of them. We may need to know more about specific kinds of people, such as working mothers, or about special problems such as the need for children's playing space, or for child care centres.

It could help social planning to know what people think about the social and physical characteristics of their environment; what their goals are and whether they intend to stay or move elsewhere; what they think about the commercial and public services in the locality, and about hospitals, schools, and transport. They may have opinions about proposed changes and they may suggest changes. From talking to people we may discover what they want — or rather, what they *think* they want; what they actually need may be another problem. We may not want fluoridisation of our water supply though dentists may say we need it; or, vice versa, we may want it and be told by other dentists that we do not need it. The possibility of conflict between what the community wants and what is needed will crop up again later. But to our democratic way of thinking it seems only right and proper to find out what people want, even if we use this information in conjunction with other information.

The idea of finding out what the consumer wants is not new. Large industrial organisations, such as car manufacturers, have been doing this for over forty years. But in social planning the practice of consulting the community is relatively new and rather rare.

In the past, social planners often neglected to consult the actual users in any way, or to consider the human and social consequences of their actions. Town planners and architects, for instance, were reluctant to study households; a few even thought that they alone knew best what was wanted. A paper published in an architects' journal saying that information from the consumers of housing might be desirable attracted this reply:

> Personally I would like to see our architects shut their ears firmly to the voice of the multitude, and quietly get on with the job that is their special province — that of planning what *they conceive* to be the best possible houses that can be built within the limits of cost laid down.[1]

This kind of detachment can create social problems. For example, the houses on one housing estate in England had L-shaped living-rooms — because of the whim of the architect, I suppose. These L-shaped rooms apparently set up tensions in the family routine; some husbands erected partitions to create a parlour-type space or sort of lounge-room. As these partitions contravened the tenancy agreement, a few timorous families took them down every week before the rent collector called.[2] The architects also sought to provide a functional separation of cooking, eating, and living, but this conflicted with the habits of the people being re-housed. Consequently, people ate at the draining boards by the sink because they thought the kitchen was the place for meals, even though it was too narrow for a table.[3] Many occupants had also changed the architect's style of decoration at some cost to themselves.[4]

The design of houses and the style of decoration should suit the convenience and taste of the occupants. In the cases just described the architects may have had good reasons for their decisions but the results were unsatisfactory for many of the occupants. These errors could have been avoided if, before the designs were finalised, an inquiry had been made into the use these people made of their houses: future occupants could have been shown layout plans and even models and asked to comment on them; perhaps preferences between alternative designs could have been assessed and some choice given in the style of decoration.

Besides the design of houses, wider social problems are involved in constructing new towns, moving people from over-crowded badly-built areas, and attracting people and industries to new or undeveloped areas. In the past mistakes have been made because the people who are to be re-housed have not been adequately studied. For example, near where I used to live in England, modern houses were built in a new area for people living in what are politely known as sub-standard areas. Because the houses were so much better, it was thought that the tenants would be willing to pay higher rents. However, on top of this the tenants now had to travel a considerable distance to work, and this was expensive. The housewife found herself a long way from the market and so, forced to shop locally, she required more for housekeeping. The result of all this was that the tenants took in lodgers, or sub-let rooms, which of course was contrary to the tenancy agreement and defeated one of the main aims of the whole scheme.[5]

Elsewhere other consequences of moving people to new areas have been observed: newcomers who are brought into existing communities experience considerable isolation[6] and the old people left behind are often lonely and uncared for.

Ageing parents often enjoy a reasonable retirement under the watchful eye of a married daughter who lives within easy visiting distance. In this way extended kinship systems provide a form of social security that is disrupted when families move to new areas and the older generation remains behind.

It is now well known that the physical arrangement of housing can influence social relationships. The relative amount of friendliness and the social pattern of friendship are both affected, for example, by the existence of cul-de-sacs or courts. One post-war American study found that on two housing projects for ex-servicemen, the distance between houses and the direction in which a house faced were two major factors affecting the development of friendship. These two factors combined to make it easy for social groups to develop within the courts.[7]

This study and others (including studies at Dagenham and Coventry in the United Kingdom) have shown that the physical arrangement is more likely to work in this way if the residents are homogeneous. If neighbours feel very different from each other and do not want to mix, such layouts may in fact produce social conflicts rather than social cohesion.[8]

There are some people, however, who prefer seclusion to sociability, and it would appear that to some extent this is a matter of social class — people in white-collar occupations show less preference for sociability than do manual workers.[9]

Quite apart then from the physical layout of the housing, neighbourly relationships are more likely to develop in the street if people have a similar social background. Moreover, a whole series of studies have shown that people *prefer* to live amongst others like themselves.[10] Should we nevertheless try to broaden their cultural experiences and outlook by intermingling houses for people of differing occupational levels?[11]

In England, the attempt to promote social mixing through town planning has failed. Of Letchworth and Welwyn it is reported that 'whatever the town planner may desire, people have a marked tendency to segregate themselves by class or income'.[12] This whole problem requires very careful consideration, but meanwhile we can do more to find out what sort of houses people prefer and what kind of a community they would like to live in.

Town-planning laws and urban development authorities now officially recognise that people should have the opportunity of voicing their opinions on planning proposals at every stage. The machinery for doing this is a matter of trial and experiment. People can be invited to attend a town-planning meeting and on the face of it this looks like 'public participation,' to which we give so much lip-service these days. But the meeting may be poorly attended, usually by people with more education and free time than most citizens; those who do attend may have special interests that they want to preserve. This is fair enough, and the meeting is intended to bring these special interests to our notice. But those who do attend will most certainly not be representative of the whole community. Mothers of young children, for example, are not likely to attend. In these circumstances it would be more democratic to conduct a survey using a representative sample.

According to Leonard England[13], public meetings on planning issues are not only unrepresentative, they tend to support the opposition only. He argues that public opinion surveys would redress the balance. They are certainly essential, even though I shall show later (p. 150) that public meetings may not always support the opposition.

The problem of social change is a particularly difficult one. People are not static either in their style of living or in their ideas. The census is one very valuable method of measuring social change, especially in the distribution and movement of the population. But the information is limited to demographic features. The census shows numerical changes but not psychological changes, for example, how patterns of social relationships are affected by population changes. Social change is also reflected in the changing attitudes of people, changes in their likes and dislikes. *Where* people live and the *kinds* of houses they live in now, may not be their ideal. Given the opportunity, they might prefer something else. In the United Kingdom one-fifth of all households move each year.[14] One survey found that people living in council housing-estates disliked the locality as much as the houses, two-thirds were dissatisfied with their houses, while more than half wanted to leave, even if the houses were repaired and improved.[15]

The problem of finding out what people want is complicated by two factors. Firstly, the majority choice should not be the sole consideration, because social planning must also make provision for the preferences of minorities as far as this is possible. And secondly, what people say they want *now* may not necessarily be the best indication of what they will want in the future. It is a question of working towards as many future options as possible. According to Pahl[16]:

> Instead of simple questions about what 'people' want, urban sociologists are now being asked by planners with increasing urgency to predict a plurality of 'good lives'. Planning for diversity and choice in new cities and regional complexes demands knowledge of the range and proportions of diversity and choice.

Pahl also reminds us how easily planners are influenced by their own utopian thinking. Planners may reject what they regard as out-dated utopias, such as Garden Cities, and unconsciously develop new ones that may or may not be related to public needs.

By using social surveys properly, planners should be able to avoid losing touch with the public they are aiming to serve. Social needs can be identified, people's wants or preferences can be assessed, and social planners can see to what extent their own thinking needs to be modified (if they are honest) and to what extent (if they are courageous) they need to educate the public regarding what could be possible. There may be alternative life-styles of which the public are as yet unaware or sceptical. We urgently need a continuous dialogue between planners and public. Direct participation in the process of planning, backed up by information from social surveys, may not be easy. The alternative is to have active planners pursuing their private utopias, and lazy ones pursuing the line of least resistance.

Social surveys can also help in evaluating the consequences of social action. Too often it is assumed that once a plan is put into effect, that is the end of the matter. For the most part, social planners have neglected to carry out follow-up studies to find out if their schemes really work. The social consequences of re-housing people from old areas have been investigated in England in Oxford and London (the references are listed at the end of this chapter) but these are notable exceptions. Much more needs to be done along similar lines, and not only in relation to housing.

Purposes of social surveys

This chapter has shown that social surveys aim to supply information for a number of different but often overlapping purposes. They may be summarised as follows.

Descriptive

1. to describe what exists — to get all the relevant facts;
2. to state the facts quantitatively;
3. to identify aspects of community life and the environment where changes seem advisable;
4. where there are known social problems, to measure the extent and characteristics of those problems.

Explanatory

5. to analyse relationships between the descriptive facts;
6. to understand what is going on (for example, population movements — such as the drift from rural to urban areas — and other social changes);
7. to identify the causes of such changes.

Predictive

8. to predict social changes;
9. to examine the merits of alternative policy proposals and action plans;
10. to predict the possible outcomes of suggested remedies for social problems.

Evaluative

— as in 9 and 10, but also —
11. to evaluate the results of past decisions (sometimes through follow-up studies);
12. to assist in modifications or adjustments suggested by the evaluation.

These are probably all the acknowledged purposes that can be identified. In addition there may be other reasons why surveys are advocated. Motives, as suggested in the next section, may differ from those assumed in this chapter.

Motives

So far I have stressed the usefulness of seeking information through social surveys. But is this why people do social surveys — to seek information? Not always. According to Stuart Rice in the foreword to P.V. Young's book *Scientific Social Surveys and Research* (1st and 2nd edns 1946, 1949), there are four main motives for conducting a social survey: a basis for planning, educational, 'magical', and tactical (gaining time). The last two may be regarded with some suspicion.

A basis for planning

Surveys provide essential information for drawing up policies and action programs. This is the motive I have mainly discussed so far, but the next can certainly also be justified.

Educational

Conducting and reporting surveys is one way of educating the public regarding social questions, policies, or the need for new legislation. For example, in Australia, until the Victorian Public Interest Research Group published its report in 1974 on the Dandenong Ranges, the general public were not aware that a popular area of distinctive natural beauty was threatened by rapid residential development. The report made it clear that regional plans and effective legislation should be drafted urgently. In other cases, surveys have probably been used to prove a need in order that a ready-made plan of action can be sold to the public. Is this always such a terrible thing to do? However good the motives might be (for instance, to improve child welfare services) we should still insist that a social survey should be carried out before a plan is finalised. The provisional plan should be flexible — or be one of several alternative plans.

'Magical'

Rice suggests that surveys may be a kind of fetish or magical rite. What might otherwise be disregarded is given respectability through statistics. Or maybe someone hopes to blind with science the unsuspecting public or even the policy-makers. One reason for this book is to increase the general understanding of what scientific social surveys can do and what are their limitations. After reading this book you will, I hope, be able to judge for yourself whether a proposed or reported survey is acceptable.

Tactical

Procrastination may be why some people or committees propose a survey; they hope to delay any decision or action. This is a real danger in the case of conservation. While a survey is being conducted to find out if the public want to protect an amenity or open space, developers may establish an irreversible advantage for their clients.

Social surveys to supplement public participation

A positive use of social surveys, embodying both the planning and the educational motives, is called for in the Skeffington Report (1969) on public participation in planning. The report acknowledges that public meetings may be unrepresentative (p. 28). The community is regarded not solely in terms of organised groups but 'as an aggregate comprising all individuals and groups' (p.1). With this in mind, the report suggests that the usual physical and land-use surveys should be supplemented by 'surveys designed to discover what people want or prefer' (p.25). Though at some stages of the discussion organised groups would certainly have an important contribution to make, a proposal regarding, say, the town centre 'affects all the inhabitants of that area and they should have the chance to say what they think' (p.26). The report continues: 'Having heard the public's wishes on the choices, or alternative strategies open to them, the authority will be able to prepare a statement of proposals.' This document will be 'based on survey material, public expression of views on the main issues and choices put to them and the authority's consideration of those views.' The report emphasises that these surveys must be on the basis of an informed public otherwise there may not be an adequate awareness of the full range of opportunities available for change and improvement (p.35).

Criticisms of social surveys

Not all social scientists are happy with the survey as a method of social inquiry. There are some who maintain that counting heads does not really tell you what is inside them. They propose instead a phenomenological approach with the emphasis on understanding people as persons and not merely as respondents who answer the questions they are asked in surveys. Various methods are favoured: they usually require a more personal relationship such as may be gained by actually living in the same community, or through participant observation (see Chapter 4). However, the phenomenological approach and the social survey are not incompatible: both can help to improve the quality of life of a community. Given sufficient time, the phenomenological approach can make a valuable contribution to a deeper understanding of the community; for immediate practical purposes we may have to rely on the more limited understanding that can be gained through social surveys. I will examine this issue more fully in the final chapter.

Notes

[1] *Journal of the Royal Institute of British Architects,* vol. 51, 1944, pp. 191-7. This is the paper by Dennis Chapman: 'Social survey technique of obtaining housing information', that provoked a letter from Elizabeth Avril published in the same journal, August 1944, pp. 269-70. In this letter she also asks: 'Is it not the community who need instruction on the proper uses of a bathroom and the proper functions of a window?' She maintains that 'the best and most genuinely admired houses of this or any other period' were built by architects who followed their own inspiration.

[2] J.M. Mogey, *Family and neighbourhood,* Oxford University Press, 1956, p. 73.

[3] *ibid.,* pp. 24-5, 74.

[4] *ibid.,* p. 25.

[5] Terence Morris, now Professor of Sociology at the London School of Economics, confirms that my account 'would reflect the position as it was at New Addington in the late 1940's and early 1950's' (personal communication). There are other examples of housing developments that failed to provide adequate accommodation for family needs, in Chapter XI, 'Delinquency, housing and social policy' in T. Morris, *The criminal area,* Routledge & Kegan Paul, London, 1957. His discussion is still relevant for social planners, though Professor Morris points out that since he wrote, housing standards have been improved and tenancy conditions radically revised.

[6]P. Willmott & M. Young, *Family and class in a London suburb,* Routledge & Kegan Paul, London, 1960, pp. 121, 123n.

[7]P. Willmott, *The evolution of a community,* Routledge & Kegan Paul, London, 1963, p. 81.

[8]*ibid.*

[9]*ibid.,* p. 80

[10]*ibid.,* pp. 112-3.

[11]See Morris, *op. cit.* pp. 186-9.

[12]Willmott, *op. cit.,* p. 114.

[13]*New Society,* 9 May 1974, p. 315.

[14]R.E. Pahl, (ed.) *Readings in urban sociology,* Pergamon Press, Oxford, 1968, p. 9.

[15]*New Society,* 25 April 1974, p. 195.

[16]Pahl, *op. cit.,* p. 17.

Further reading

Many of the references given in this chapter come from the following books (full details of which are given in the References, p. 159):

Mogey, 1956; Young & Willmott, 1957; Willmott & Young, 1960; and Willmott, 1963. These books illustrate the usefulness of survey methods and make challenging reading for anyone interested in the social consequences of re-housing people from old areas.

Chapter 2
Types of Social Surveys

Surveys can be classified broadly according to their general purposes; they are descriptive, explanatory, predictive, or evaluative as discussed in Chapter 1. Motives are less obvious and do not provide a sound basis for classification. It is more usual to classify surveys according to their methods or type of information. Thus the survey might be an interview survey or a postal inquiry; in either case it could be a sample survey or it could aim to include everybody. I will deal with methods of collecting data and of sampling subjects in later chapters. Here, I have grouped surveys according to the nature of the information being sought. This is to show the variety and wide range of information that can be sought in surveys, and the different levels of difficulty in obtaining that information.

The classifications used here are implicit in Chapter 1: survey information may tell us who the people are, how well off they are, what they do, and what they think. In more formal terms, a survey may collect data on the demographic characteristics of people in the area, or their social and economic state, or their activities, or their opinions.

Type no. 1. Demographic characteristics of people in a defined area

This is perhaps the least difficult type of survey because it seeks the kind of information usually covered by a census; for example, the composition of the family or the household, and such items as marital status, age, number of children, number of school-children in the area. These items are reasonably factual, and answers will be objective and accurate with some exceptions. For example, people may not wish to let a casual inquirer know all about some aspects of the household.

The overall accuracy can be checked against other sources, such as census data. Then why not just use census tables? For two reasons: firstly, as already explained, we may require information that is more recent than the previous census; secondly, we may need the demographic information for subsequent analysis (for example, to correlate demographic characteristics with attitudes recorded during the survey). We may wish to know if older people or married couples think differently on various issues than those who are younger or single (the so-called 'response patterns').

Type no. 2.   Social and economic conditions

This includes information that could indicate whether people are well off, barely comfortable, or below the poverty line. Some of the first social surveys were concerned with poverty, for example, Booth in London, 1886-1902,[1] and Rowntree in York, United Kingdom, 1901 and in the 1930s[2]. Recently, poverty surveys have been carried out in Melbourne. But surveys in this type are not restricted to poverty; they often attempt to produce scales or social indices based on questions about level of education, occupation, income, house ownership or tenancy, and housing conditions. Type 2 would also include surveys concerned with aspects of the social environment such as health and hospital facilities, schools and recreation, shopping and transport, and other social amenities.

These surveys are more difficult than the purely demographic inquiries. Though still reasonably factual and objective, at least in theory, in practice some bias or errors are likely. Cross-checking becomes more difficult but (as in Type 1) some idea of the overall accuracy may be gained by checking against other sources. Some direct observation may be necessary — of housing conditions, state of repairs and building maintenance, and local amenities. Items relating to the social environment may overlap with Type 3 which covers what people do.

Type no. 3.   Activities

This usually means what people do other than working for a living, though it could include any work in or around the house — domestic work as well as hobbies, painting the house, and gardening. It could include questions about travelling to work, visiting friends and relations, getting to schools and shops; questions about going to church, playing or watching sport, and general leisure activities. How much time is spent listening to radio, watching television, and reading newspapers — and when?

Financial expenditure on travelling, entertainment and various items of shopping might also be of interest. In many ways, especially as regards expenditure items, these surveys resemble what is done in market research or consumer surveys.

Obviously this type of inquiry is even more difficult than the previous two types. So much depends on the respondent's memory; people are often inaccurate when asked how much time or money they spend on various activities. Instead of expecting a quick reply on the doorstep, giving people more time to answer might help to improve accuracy.

Then again it is well known that people tend to over-estimate some activities (like how often they go to church) and under-estimate others (such as drinking in hotel bars or pubs). This happens when people give answers that they think conform to social expectations. If this tendency is widespread it can produce response bias towards social acceptability (or social desirability) — a problem that I will tackle in Chapter 5.

However, providing the questions are direct and clearly stated, they are not impossible to answer since they refer to actualities in the respondent's recent experience. It can be much more difficult to ask and to answer questions in the next group.

Type number 4. Opinions and attitudes

At first it may seem puzzling why this is often regarded as the most difficult kind of inquiry. After all, we are usually proud of our opinions and declare we have a right to them, and (though not always) that we don't mind who knows what we think. However, to declare: 'This is a free country, isn't it?' means for some people that they have the right to keep their opinions to themselves — which of course they have. For others it means the right to let anyone know what they think, so they should welcome people asking them. Often what we call our 'own' opinion is merely what we have read in the newspapers that morning; this may partly explain why opinions vary from day to day. Perhaps the right to our own opinions is really the right to choose our opinions from sources that we regard as both expert and trustworthy.

By 'attitudes' we usually mean something rather more stable than fluctuating opinions. A related set of opinions reasonably consistent in their meanings and intentions, as well as reasonably consistent over a period of time (at least a few months one would expect) could be regarded as an attitude. In addition there is usually a consistent value judgment entailed in the opinions and at least a hint of how a person might act or wish to act in certain social situations. Behaviour may not always be in accordance with the supposed or stated attitude, but that is another problem. We might of course ask, in that case, which is the *true* attitude — what a person says or what that person does in the actual situation?

Racial prejudice is one kind of attitude; political, religious, and nationalist attitudes are other examples. In recent years a new kind of attitude towards the environment has emerged — the conservationist attitude. Its strength will need to be assessed along with considerations of economic and ecological balance whenever the development or re-development of towns and land is under public scrutiny.

Related to our attitudes, either as part of them or as a compromise between conflicting attitudes, are personal preferences. Somewhat infrequently people are asked where they would like to live, as in Melbourne once[3] or how they like living in tall buildings[4].

Mixed types

Few surveys keep strictly within one of the four types described above.

Coverage of surveys

A survey can cover a few case studies, any number of invited volunteers, a systematic sample, or all those in the area to be surveyed as in a census. In former years a census was usually a complete enumeration; however in some countries a sample census is now used either as a trial run or to gather representative information between normal census years. A 10 per cent sample was used for the 1966 Population Census of the United Kingdom.

The term **population** means all the people or objects under investigation before any sample is drawn; in other words, the census population or, as in sample surveys, the population from which the sample is taken. Thus the population may consist of all the houses or all the housewives in Karlville; all the shops or the shopkeepers in Collingbourne; or all the users of the local car park or public parks. This is often referred to as the **survey population** meaning the population actually covered whether in total or by sampling. Unless there are complicating factors, the survey population should correspond exactly to the **target population** which is the population that the survey aims to cover. But circumstances may prevent this. Some units of the target population may be inaccessible, and others may not be listed so that they have no chance of being in the sample. In such cases the coverage of the survey must be regarded as incomplete.

Parameters are the characteristics of the survey population; they may be **attributes** (such as race and religion) or **variables** (such as age, income, and distance from work) and can be stated as totals, proportions, or averages.

The parameters of a problem refer to the relevant population characteristics and not to the boundaries, extent, or outer limits of the problem; this mistake arises from a confusion with 'perimeter'. The actual value of a parameter may be an unknown quantity though sometimes it can be obtained from census information. When the value of an attribute or variable is calculated from a sample, the result is called a **statistic.** In effect a statistic is an estimate of a parameter obtained through a sample.

A sample is not merely any part of the population; it is the part of the population that is selected by statistically sound methods. The question of how one draws a sample from the defined population and how one decides on a systematic basis who or what is going to form part of the sample, must be left for a later chapter. Meanwhile it is worth noting that asking for volunteers is not the same as asking systematically selected individuals if they would mind answering a few questions. If volunteers are called for, or if people are allowed to volunteer without first being systematically selected, the sample will be **self-selected.** This has many disadvantages since these self-selected volunteers are not usually representative of the population in some important characteristics. For example, they are often better educated and have more leisure than the average person in the population. And they may have a special interest in the topic to be investigated. Thus, conservationists will readily volunteer if the activities of the local quarry are the main subject of the inquiry.

Surveys and research

The word 'research' is often used in referring to a survey (as in the Skeffington Report), but a distinction can be made between social surveys and social research (P.V. Young, 1966). Surveys are more concerned with treating and preventing social problems than with formulating theories and laws. Surveys may be used to find out what is wrong and, if necessary, to arouse public opinion with a view to reaching a solution. They may also be used to measure public opinion in order to shape public policy.

Social survey research is in another category and is usually concerned with the logic and method of social surveys. Many examples of this kind will be found in the *Public Opinion Quarterly.*

Notes

[1]C. Booth, (ed.) *Labour and life of the people of London,* 17 vols, Macmillan, London, 1889-1902.

[2]B.S. Rowntree, *Poverty: a study of town life,* Macmillan, London, 2nd edn 1902; and, by the same author, *Poverty and progress: a second social survey of York,* Longmans Green, London, 1941.

[3]H. Stretton, *Ideas for Australian cities,* Georgian House, Melbourne, 1973, p. 199.

[4]A. Stevenson, E. Martin, & J. O'Neill, *High living: a study of family life in flats,* Melbourne University Press, 1967.

Further reading

The Australian poverty survey is an excellent example of a systematic study covering a difficult topic. The careful methods used in sampling and interviewing are of general interest and would be applicable to other problems. The survey and methods are described in Henderson, Harcourt & Harper, 1970.

Quite a different approach was adopted by a research team of social workers (Stevenson, Martin & O'Neill, 1967) who wished to find out what Housing Commission tenants in Melbourne thought about their experiences of living in high-density flats. The study does not claim to be a piece of rigorously designed research, as the authors admit on page 135. But it does provide a descriptive background that could be a useful guide for more systematic investigations. The authors avoid 'the application of elaborate statistical techniques to data that are unsuitable for such treatment'. Instead, their qualitative approach has produced a very readable account, which is full of human warmth.

A useful introduction to urban sociology, which draws examples from all over the world is Pahl's chapter 'A perspective on urban sociology' in Pahl, 1968, pp. 3-44. I most warmly endorse Pahl's final reminder that our contribution to society will depend on the quality rather than the quantity of social information provided by surveys.

There are fewer reports of surveys in rural areas, perhaps because the population is so scattered. Worthwhile Australian studies include Oeser & Emery, 1954. A later work by Emery & Oeser (1958) is a study of how technical and other information reaches farmers through official and unofficial sources. For the United Kingdom, see Stacey, 1960.

Full-length articles reporting the results of social surveys frequently appear in the British weekly *New Society*. In addition there are brief summaries, citing references, of works that have appeared elsewhere. For example, we read in *New Society* vol. 29, no. 623, 1974, p. 681 that middle-class people are more concerned with their environment than are working-class people. Apparently in Market Drayton, Shropshire, England, concern for the environment is an overwhelmingly middle-class affair, according to a 1971 study reported by B. Goodchild in *Urban Studies*, vol. 11, no. 2, 1974, pp. 157-69.

The historical aspects of surveys are covered in Young, 4th edn, 1966. A brief account will be found in Abrams, 1951.

Chapter 3

Planning the Survey

It is essential to work according to a well thought out plan otherwise the report will not be ready in time. A draft plan can be prepared fairly quickly by experienced social surveyors, but preliminary information must be obtained, and many decisions will have to be made before the final plan can be settled. Objectives will have to be discussed and decisions made about the most suitable methods to obtain the maximum relevant information with the time and money available.

This chapter is in two parts. The first part describes in detail the extensive exploratory work and provisional decisions needed before the final plan is made; this part takes up most of the chapter. The second part briefly lists the steps for which adequate time must be allowed in the final plan.

Social surveys are principally about people: who they are, how they live, what they do, and what they think about their lives and the society in which they live. People vary: the survey method used in one city may not suit another city; problems and solutions are seldom transferable; questions asked in one place may be meaningless or have different connotations in another place; even the words used differ — a lavatory may be a 'loo' or a 'dunny', depending on where you are. Any survey that does not allow sufficient time for preliminary exploration and discussion is in danger of wasting time and resources at a later stage.

1 Preliminary steps before making the final plan

(a) Familiarisation with the problem in general

It can be misleading, and in some cases actually harmful, to suppose that a researcher should begin fieldwork with an open mind, if by this is really meant an empty mind. Certainly he should remain unbiased at all times, but not clueless. You can hardly follow up a clue if you cannot recognise one when you see it. Therefore the very first thing that must be done is to find out what is already known, and what relevant surveys are being done or being planned elsewhere. This means reading relevant studies and reports, and having discussions with experts. One should lead to the other so that experts will suggest what should be read, and the reading material can indicate which experts to seek. Sometimes there will be a kind of chain reaction. One expert will suggest another, he will suggest a reference, and so on.

Some of the relevant studies may have been carried out in other localities or even in different countries; local studies may already be a few years old. Obviously it is dangerous to generalise from these results. Nevertheless you can learn from the method used, and the studies may suggest issues that should be explored in your survey.

At the same time you could be having talks with key informants. These are people who are not necessarily experts in the academic sense, but who because of their jobs or special positions know the district or some elements of the problem. It may be necessary to be aware of any possible bias in what they have to say and this is where preparation through reading and discussion will help. However in the absence of relevant studies or experts, a researcher may have to begin with key informants. In one local study that was concerned with the possible demolition or preservation of dwelling houses milk-bar owners proved to be fountains of information because customers talked to them about what was going on in the neighbourhood. In another study, a priest was able to describe many of the problems that the local aged residents faced in their daily lives.

Sometimes, in order to sharpen the issues involved, it is actually an advantage to talk to people who are obviously biased. The secretaries of local sports clubs are usually keen to preserve playing fields and to increase the area available for sport and recreation. But their knowledge of local conditions can be useful. Similarly, local conservationists will have strong views and may suggest possibilities that would otherwise be left out of a survey.

As a result of all this reading and talking, together with some essential local observation, it should be possible to formulate a preliminary analysis of the situation —

> what kind of survey is required?
> what are the important issues?
> what are the kinds of questions that need to be asked?

(b) *Further exploratory work*

On the basis of the preliminary analysis you are now ready to carry out an exploratory pilot study. For this you must select people who form part of the population you intend to survey. Be as informal as possible: the style of interviewing should resemble an ordinary conversation. Your aim should be to discover how *they* see the issues; what aspect is important to them; and what kind of language, concepts, phrases, they use when referring to these issues.

For exploratory purposes 'open' questions are best. One or two like these —

> What are the things you like about Parktown?
> What do you dislike about Parktown?
> What are some of the changes you would like to see here?
> Why did you decide to come here?
> Would you prefer to live somewhere else?

At this stage you can ring the changes on the questions — try one here and another there — try different wording. In the final survey this variation would ruin the comparability of the replies and invalidate your data. But in exploratory work you need a flexible approach in order to see things the way others do and at the same time collect some specific information relating to your main problem. This can be done by narrowing the focus of the conversation in the following manner.

> How often do you walk to the local shops?
> How long does it take you to get there?
> If they built a swimming pool in Collingbourne, how often do you think you (the members of your family) would go there?

The number of people you interview at this stage will depend on how much time you have and how much variation there is in the response patterns. Usually something between twenty and thirty is enough — after that replies tend to become repetitious and nothing much new emerges.

At each stage you must keep asking yourself 'is a survey necessary?' Perhaps the same information can be obtained by another method, for example by analysing existing records or by direct observation. If you hope to show cause-and-effect relationships an experiment may be more efficient or indeed essential. In that case it may be necessary to conduct two surveys at different points of time or to compare two areas. For example, the effects of television on leisure patterns could be studied by surveying an area before and after the introduction of television (allowing a suitable time to pass between the two occasions). Alternatively, a comparison of leisure activities could be made by taking one area with television and another without, providing the areas are similar in all other respects — an almost impossible proviso.

(c) *Selecting specific objectives*

What kind of information is required? In the previous chapter the discussion on types of social surveys outlined four main groups — demographic, social conditions, activities, and opinions. The selection of specific objectives within these groups will be guided by common sense and your exploratory work. In some rare cases a little theory might help.

In market research and in management consultancy it is thought unwise (it could even be disastrous) to assume that the client knows precisely what the problem is and which questions to ask. Management may be thinking in terms of increasing sales of existing products by intensive advertising when they should be considering other possibilities such as producing alternative ranges, or reducing the cost of the article, or reducing the range and streamlining production. Similarly a local government may prematurely select a problem before considering other possibilities.

In any kind of commissioned survey the client's real needs are paramount and considerable exploratory work and discussion are essential in order to discover what these are. But these needs take precedence over interesting theoretical issues. In 'basic' research surveys, however, the theoretical requirements come first. It has been argued that the best design for a basic research project is not necessarily the best design for the same project in applied research and that the two types of research have differing requirements that entail different designs[1].

Typically a social survey will include questions that are thought to indicate level of social class or social status. The hierarchical rank order implied in such terms as upper, middle, and lower (or working) class contains a social class discrimination and even an element of snobbery which many people find objectionable. The term Socio-Economic Status (referred to as SES) may indeed identify the same concept but was intended to be a scientifically neutral, unemotional term. Social classification is often made, for survey purposes, on the basis of one item such as occupation, income, level of education, or area of residence. These usually produce closely similar rank orders (that is, they are highly correlated) and nothing much is gained by trying to combine them into a single index of social status. In fact each of these items should be regarded as a matter of interest in its own right without assuming any general scale. There is not much point in showing that the children of middle-class families do better at school than working-class children, without asking why. The relationship of a general scale of social status to school performance is the beginning and not the end of the inquiry. The operative factors could be the mother's level of education, the number of books in the home, and the extent to which the family uses the local library.

Sometimes, for sampling purposes, a general scale of social status can be useful; different areas can be selected, matched, compared, or sampled according to social status levels. There is available in Australia, for instance, a list of 611 census collectors' districts in and around Melbourne. The status score and rank order of each district was calculated on the basis of 24 characteristics derived from the 1961 census data. Occupational factors (21 items) dominate the index; house ownership (one item) and education (two items) make up the rest[2]. For Sydney a different method was used by Congalton[3]: public opinion ratings of the social standing of Sydney suburbs were collected to form a status ranking list.

In the USA a socio-economic index for male occupations has been constructed by Duncan, based on prestige, education, and income[4]. Occupations have also been ranked according to the public's opinion of their prestige in Australia[5], and in the United Kingdom, there is the Hall-Jones Scale of Occupational Prestige for males. Both the American and British occupational scales are reproduced in an appendix by Oppenheim[6]. Social classifications used in official censuses are also available for social surveys.

One final point on the selection of specific objectives. It may seem convenient to use the same items or seek information comparable to other surveys. If there is something to be gained by comparing results from different surveys, this is justified; but not if the only motive is to save time and preliminary work. There is no point in seeking information on social class, religion, or anything that is not going to be used in the analysis. Think carefully how you are going to use the information when you get it.

(d) Choice of methods

Depending on the selection of specific objectives, a number of methodological decisions will have to be made.

How is the information to be obtained? This can be done either by direct observation or by asking people questions through the mail with questionnaires or in personal interviews (or by a combination of methods). Different types of interviews will be selected according to circumstances.

How are the respondents to be selected? First you must formulate a precise definition of the relevant population — all residents or only adult female residents? all families or only families with school children? and so on. Notice that in the first case the unit of population will be one person and in the second case the unit will be a group of people.

Next a suitable sampling frame must be found which lists or contains all members of the relevant population. Ideally it should contain each and every unit once, but *only* once. In many areas a telephone directory would be a very incomplete sampling frame.

Then the method of sampling must be chosen and a decision made about the intended size of the sample. The help of a statistician at this stage may prevent many mistakes later.

This sequence is somewhat theoretical. In practice we tend to move back and forth from one step to another until a reasonable solution is reached.

What statistical analyses will be required? These will depend on the specific objectives, plus a not unreasonable modicum of scientific curiosity. But the prospective analysis will affect the format of the questions and response categories that still have to be worked out. If it is intended to use computer facilities, this could also affect the contents and layout of the interview schedule or questionnaire; a computer specialist should be consulted at the earliest opportunity.

Detailed consideration of the relative merits of different methods of collecting data, sampling methods, and analysis will appear in subsequent chapters. For present purposes it is sufficient to say that these decisions will have to be made, at least tentatively, before drawing up a time schedule for the survey, which is the next step.

2   Final or overall plan — time schedule

This is mainly a question of estimating the time required for each step and the total cost of the survey. The costs will include printing the questionnaires or interview schedules; postage and stationery; typing and clerical assistance; payment for interviews; travelling expenses; computer services (card punching, programming, computer time); printing the final report.

The time schedule must allow adequate time for each step or phase in the survey along the following lines.

(a) *Drafting* the questionnaire or interview guide.

(b) *Pre-test* to check the suitability of the wording of the questions and the proposed response categories. Failure to do this properly may lead to delays later, for example in the second revision.

(c) *First revision* and printing of sufficient copies for the pilot survey.

(d) *Interviewers* — selection and training.

(e) *Pilot survey* or trial run. This is a small-scale dress rehearsal of the main survey. Subjects must be selected in accordance with the proposed sampling procedure; questions must be asked in exactly the manner prescribed for the survey. This is not an exploratory phase. It is intended as a strict test of the survey design and data instruments. Therefore the standard procedure must be used in every detail. The specific points on which the pilot survey will provide essential guidance are discussed in Moser and Kalton[7].

(f) *Second revision.* It may be apparent that some questions were misunderstood or skipped; interviewers may relate that they had difficulties with certain items. Unless extensive revision and re-printing is required, the final survey can follow in a few days. Thorough pre-testing as in (b) pays off.

(g) *The survey*. This will be the time you've dreaded, or eagerly anticipated — the fieldwork — the collection of data.

(h) *Analysing the data.*

(i) *Writing the report.*

With a short inquiry and some luck each step might take only a day and the whole study could be completed in two weeks. But a more substantial survey would run closer to two months. When planning your time schedule don't forget to allow for public holidays and weekends.

After the time schedule and cost budget have been set out, some kind of cost-benefit analysis is required. Then consider the usefulness of the results and their possible applications.

Review the time factor and the costs for each item before you consult your client or whoever made the request for the survey. Finally, decide whether the survey should go ahead.

Notes

[1]See D.S. Tull & G.S. Albaum, *Survey research: A decisional approach,* International Textbooks, Aylesbury, UK, 1973.

[2]F.L. Jones, 'A social ranking of Melbourne suburbs', *Australian and New Zealand Journal of Sociology,* vol. 3, October 1967, pp. 93-110.

[3]A.A. Congalton, *Status and prestige in Australia,* Cheshire, Melbourne, 1969.

[4]Albert J. Reiss Jr, *Occupations and social status,* Free Press, New York, 1961.

[5]Congalton *op. cit.*

[6]A.N. Oppenheim, *Questionnaire design and attitude measurement,* Basic Books, New York, 1966.

[7]C.A. Moser & G. Kalton, *Survey methods in social investigation,* Heinemann, London, 2nd edn, 1971, pp. 48-51.

Further reading

The standard reference (as for everything else in this book) is Moser and Kalton, 1971. At this point you should find their first three chapters easy and useful. Chapter 2 is specifically on the planning of social surveys.

There are two earlier books that will take you much further than mine: they are Goode and Hatt, 1952, and Hyman, 1955. You could dip into them now but you might prefer to read them when you have finished this book.

Oppenheim, 1966, has a useful first chapter on 'Problems of Survey Design' though I would question whether he was wise in making the aims and hypotheses the first step.

Chapter 4

Observation

Science, we are often told, begins with observation. Dramatic instances in the history of science seem to confirm that casual observation may lead to important discoveries. Archimedes observed what happened to the water when he stepped into his bath. Newton noticed an apple fall to the ground and Watt saw the lid of the kettle pushed up by the steam. But it is almost certain that observations that have led to scientific discoveries were not entirely casual. Moreover, if science begins with observation, it does not end there though it may return to further observation for validation.

Science ends with casual observation for all those people who imagine that what they claim to have seen is scientific fact. The unreliability of eyewitnesses is well known. That is the paradox. Observation is the basis for science but observation is notoriously biased and inaccurate. We need to understand both the usefulness and the limitations of observation.

Purposes of observation

Familiarisation — getting to know the locale

Before we can ask meaningful questions about any place, we need to know what it is like in general. We need to know something about its physical characteristics and appearance; types of buildings, streets, and open spaces. We also need to observe, as far as it is possible, what kind of people live there, work there, or come there for shopping and so on. On the basis of our own observations, we will be in a better position to understand what people are talking about when we begin our preliminary discussions with them.

Preliminary assessment

Though initially our reactions will be highly subjective, we can form some idea of what is typical of the area. We can make a special note of the exceptions or anything unusual. This may be useful for our subsequent questions.

This preliminary assessment is purely tentative. We must avoid jumping to conclusions before we have compared different kinds of observations and checked these against the local viewpoint. A street of broken fences, cracked windows and tattered curtains should not cause us to write off the district as a slum that has to be pulled down and replaced with modern buildings. Touring the district by car (the windscreen survey) has its uses, particularly if the area is large, but it is no substitute for doorstep contacts, or better still, invitations to come inside and have a talk.

Formulating hypotheses

If we keep an open mind, prepared to let a place 'talk' to us instead of imposing on it our own preconceived ideas, then our observations will suggest possible hypotheses for testing later. These first approximate hypotheses might explain the regular features or any unusual features and exceptions. Other hypotheses might explain any changing features or absence of change.

Many of our proposed explanations will be based on common sense and may seem rather unexciting at this stage. Nevertheless they may serve as good working hypotheses that will help to provide some direction and enable us to be more systematic in planning our survey.

We may even have the good fortune of being blessed with some serendipity (the faculty of making happy and unexpected discoveries by chance — possibly when we are looking for something else).

To observe actual behaviour

First-hand knowledge of what people actually do in certain situations may lead us to question the veracity of reported behaviour. If there are strong social pressures to behave in specified ways, people may be reluctant to talk about their own or other people's infringements of these codes. Actual social behaviour may not always be the same as socially approved behaviour.

Problems involved in observation

There are only two basic ways in which we can investigate human behaviour. We can watch people or we can ask them questions (in an interview or by questionnaire). It may sound easy to tell an investigator to go and see for himself, but there are several problems.

When an observer is watching another person or persons there is the possibility of error arising at both ends of the 'telescope'. Consider first the errors that arise because the observer is human.

Errors of Observation — Type 1 (the observer)

1.   It is humanly impossible for one person to observe everybody or everything that is going on. Therefore a selection has to be made; we decide to observe certain features and events, and to disregard others. The behaviour of dogs in the car park may seem irrelevant and can be ignored. On second thoughts, it could be important. How do we select what is to be observed?

The work of previous investigators, some common sense with a dash of imagination (even a little theory) could help guide the selection. But we must always remember to keep alert for new possibilities.

2.   Some observers are quite clearly biased. They may believe that cars are a menace to civilisation or that the official town plan is the best that can be devised. Since people tend to see what they want to see, their biased observations are likely to support their preconceptions — or their prejudices (to use a stronger, more emotive word, thus disclosing a bias against other people's biases!).

This type of bias is fairly easily recognised and can be counterbalanced. The observer may even be aware of his own bias in some respects. Unconscious bias is more subtle: a middle-class girl may describe curtains as 'dirty' when they are quite clean but discoloured.

3.   We very rarely, if ever, observe life in the raw. We are human beings and not cameras, and we come to any situation with a vast wealth of previous experience. We 'know' what is going on when we watch, instead of merely seeing or observing[1].

The need to draw inferences or to interpret what is going on around us is part of a very strong psychological process — understanding the environment so that we can cope with it. We do not say 'that frowning man is approaching me with clenched fists'; we say 'that angry man is trying to frighten me'.

Actually, drawing inferences is a very economical way of observing. There just is not time to observe every trivial detail of an action, let alone write it all down.

How can we keep out unwarranted inferences? How can inference be kept to a minimum? Who is to make the inferences? These are difficult questions which highlight the need for careful training, and for some decision as to whether inferences may be left to the observer in the field or whether they must remain the task of the research director.

There is no simple solution that will cover every case in advance. Bertrand Russell's classic example of the difference between *observation* and *inference* has often been cited and is still worth reading.

4.   Recording notes of your observations is another problem. This can be very time-consuming and that is why we tend to record inferences rather than detailed lengthy descriptions. The solution is to use clearly defined schedules and categories, and systematic methods of recording. In

exploratory work the categories must not be too restrictive or something important might be missed.

The other problem about taking notes is that recording can interfere with observing. You cannot watch and write at the same time unless you are highly skilled. In these situations, speaking into a tape-recorder might help, providing your subjects cannot hear you. Football commentators manage to follow the game and describe it simultaneously with only a few seconds time-lag between event and spoken words. Their 'subjects' cannot hear them however. Our problem is how to take notes without being conspicuous observers. We may have to rely on our fallible memory. Otherwise we may affect the events we are supposed to be watching passively.

WHAT CAN YOU SEE?

You say, 'What can you see on the horizon?' One man says, 'I see a ship.' Another says, 'I see a steamer with two funnels.' A third says, 'I see a Cunarder going from Southampton to New York.' How much of what these three people say is to count as perception? They may all three be perfectly right in what they say, and yet we should not concede that a man can 'perceive' that the ship is going from Southampton to New York. This, we should say, is inference. But it is by no means easy to draw the line; some things which are, in an important sense, inferential, must be admitted to be perceptions. The man who says 'I see a ship' is using inference. Apart from experience, he only sees a queerly shaped dark dot on a blue background. Experience has taught him that that sort of dot 'means' a ship.[2]

5.   Unsystematic observation is very much a question of chance, though not pure or random chance. Hence we may be mistaken in thinking that our observations are typical or representative. Our observation posts will probably be selected on a rational or purposive basis — the market, railway station, main cross-roads and so on. It depends on what kind of activities we hope to observe. But the time we find convenient may be unrepresentative of the normal level and type of activity. We can get round this problem with **time sampling**; units of time are regarded as belonging to a 'population' and sampled accordingly.

6.   One final problem of observer error is not being there when something interesting happens! For example, at certain times of the year

and on certain days, the narrow roads in England's Lake District are choked with motorists. Fortunately as there are permanent resident observers (the National Park wardens) these events are well-known. But a casual observer, choosing wrong days, might conclude that there is no traffic problem in the Lake District.

How to be present when the events to be studied actually occur, is not usually a serious problem unless the researcher is particularly interested in race riots or the industrial pollution of rivers. But traffic infringements might escape our observational net; so might flash floods, and the handling of emergencies such as fires and street accidents.

Solutions

Some of these problems can be overcome by adopting procedures such as —

A division of labour: using more than one observer, or teams of observers on each location; different aspects are allocated to different observers who can then concentrate on special features without having to see everything.

Training observers: until a suitable level of consistency or reliability is reached.

Categorisation: using clearly defined schedules with pre-determined check-list items for speed of recording.

Time sampling: and if necessary, location sampling.

Errors of observation — Type 2 (the effects)

It is well known that people who know they are being observed do not behave normally, though it is worth pointing out here that behaving differently in private and in public is perfectly normal! Parents do not swear at their children on 'open days' at school. Motorists do not ignore pedestrian crossings if a policeman is present. In general, the problem is to observe people without affecting the behaviour we are attempting to observe. Consider, for example, to what extent it might be difficult or impossible to carry out an investigation into the use people make of their own private gardens, through direct observation.

The effects of being observed include —

1. Embarrassment: decreased skill of performance or lowered activity. People may talk less, or leave.

2. Showing off: performing above normal, attracting attention, trying to be funny.

3. Increased motivation: not just showing off, but an increased interest in their own activity just because other people appear to be interested. In industry social scientists refer to this as the 'Hawthorne effect'[3].

4. Suppression: socially disapproved behaviour — swearing, fighting, gambling, traffic code infringements — all diminish during observation. One day people may even feel guilty about throwing down litter, or letting their dogs foul public footpaths.

5. Suspicion: an observer who arouses suspicion might find the police investigating him! But people may well wonder: 'Why am I being watched?' and the observer has no opportunity to explain the purpose of the investigation.

Methods designed to overcome these effects. 1. Unobtrusive observation. In some situations, such as in the experimental laboratory, in clinics and in schools it is possible to use one-way vision screens. Some establishments such as banks, shops, art galleries and museums, now use closed-circuit TV cameras for security reasons. Presumably this method could be used in social survey research but the equipment would be expensive.

By placing themselves in suitable positions observers can unobtrusively watch the behaviour of pedestrians and motorists, children crossing roads near schools, the parking of cars, local congestion as people arrive or leave their places of employment, and people shopping. (Once lunch-time traffic and shoppers in Melbourne were observed from a helicopter. This caused even more congestion — a helicopter is hardly an unobtrusive instrument of observation!)

Several attempts have been made to find new unobtrusive methods of measuring behaviour in order to infer the strength of various attitudes. These include the lost-letter technique[4] and other ingenious devices. Though they might be useful for indicating prevalent attitudes in and around given areas, it is not always possible to define the subject population with accuracy.

2. Participant observation. The observer becomes a member of the community (or already may be an existing member) and participates in activities and social interactions. By living in the community, or taking up a job in the locality or an acceptable role such as secretary of the sports club, the observer experiences events in much the same way as the local residents do, from the inside and not as an outsider. This makes the experiences much more meaningful. The observer feels the stresses and strains of social situations, enjoys the satisfactions and suffers the frustrations of the environment.

Initially, to gain experience or to get background material for a play or a book, the participant observer may let the stream of life carry him along and make no attempt to meet everybody nor to sample every possible situation. He records his observations mainly according to the things that strike him as interesting. He does not use systematic categories to classify his various experiences or what people say, and probably does not keep count of anything in particular. He just lives the life. A detailed diary, full of illustrative descriptions and accounts of his own and other people's reactions, would be the main record kept.[5]

However, by sampling and by systematically recording data, the participant observer could introduce a degree of standardisation. But he must keep a reasonable balance between behaving naturally and behaving like a systematic social scientist. This problem underlines the paradox of participant observation. The aim of giving full scope to *subjective* experience, getting the 'feel' of the situation from the inside, can easily conflict with the *objectivity* desired by the scientist. Participation helps to break down the barriers in interpersonal communication. The resulting rapport can become so warm that objectivity is lost. The participant observer then joins sides with his informants and sees things only from their point of view. It then becomes difficult for him to remain objective and to observe events without influencing them.

This is the paradox of the dual purpose of participant observation:

Subjective richness, gained from participating, becoming involved, and behaving naturally

versus

Objective accuracy, gained from observing systematically, remaining at heart somewhat aloof, and striving to observe events without influencing them (not even by one's participation).

To avoid causing important changes in the behaviour under study, the participant observer may find it necessary to conceal the fact that systematic observations are being made. This can be done by openly adopting a role such as 'social historian'[6], or occupying a position such as barman in a public house[7].

In this way the observer hopes to become part of the furniture of the place, moved around but not moving others. Or if you prefer, a kind of super fly on the wall, noticing everything but remaining unnoticed.

Concealed participation, also known as disguised participation, was the method chosen by a group of social scientists who joined a peculiar religious group in order to observe them from within. The real members of the group believed that they were in touch with the infinite and would soon be rescued from a cataclysmic flood by some flying saucers that would arrive from outer space[8]. Disguised participation may seem like spying and for this reason ethical objections to the method have been raised. There are many less dramatic examples of disguised participant observation.

One difficulty with the method in general is that participant observers can only mix with a small porportion of the community. To study the origin of a community and the quality of suburban life, through personal experience, Gans and his wife lived in a New Jersey suburb for the first two years of its existence, 1958-60. Though their observations ranged much wider, they could only participate in one group, the people living in the block[9]. By having a team of participant observers, occupying roles at different social levels in the community, this difficulty could be overcome.

3. Indirect observation through the use of records. If the records have been collected over a period of time before the investigator made known any interest, then there is no risk of influencing the behaviour thus recorded. The disadvantage is that the records may not be in the form most convenient for research purposes[10].

It is essential to know how the figures were collected, what method of sampling (if any) was used, and how the categories were defined. During the relevant period these definitions may have changed; hence the problem of comparing statistics for juvenile delinquency, to take one example. The boundaries of the areas recorded may also have changed at times and may not coincide with the defined area to be surveyed.

Usually the researcher has no control over the manner, accuracy, and consistency with which the records have been collected. With regard to church attendance, for instance, it has been suggested that in common with religious beliefs and practices generally, 'the facts about present apathy are far more precise than the facts about past fervour'[11]. Is the alleged decline in church attendance an observable or a recorded fact, or is it an unsubstantiated impression?

Leaving aside the use of records we have the following classificaion of observational methods:

Experimental
(not usual in social surveys)
Naturalistic
non-participant — the watcher on the side-lines.
    (i) concealed
    (ii) obvious (e.g. staff making a traffic census on street corners).
Participant — four forms:

	Concealed or Disguised	Open or Undisguised
Controlled or Systematic	1	2
Uncontrolled, Unsystematic	3	4

The usefulness of observation

Direct observation is often neglected when it could be a valuable method. Unless one is measuring opinions and attitudes on topics and in populations with which one is already familiar, observation of some kind is essential in the exploratory phase of the survey. Fairly casual and unsystematic observation can provide useful insights. But observation of this kind is a method of discovery, not a method of proof. If observation is chosen as the main method of data collection, then a more rigorous, controlled and systematic style must be used.

The failure to use observation more often is probably due to the limitation in the range of people and events that can be covered. However, observation has proved to be most valuable for studying small communities in action, how people live and behave, especially in relatively 'closed' areas. Observation is also most suitable for studying the physical aspects of a locality, the type of materials used in buildings, distances between houses and from house to street, and the adequacy of footpaths. The physical conditions of supposedly sub-standard areas could hardly be studied without direct observation. The study of traffic conditions, parking facilities for shoppers and pedestrian congestion would also require observation. Rather than interview young children, it would be better to watch them crossing streets and playing in open spaces.

As already stated, observation is limited in range, and the accuracy depends on the observer's interpretation of visual impressions. There are problems in sampling public behaviour, which are only partly overcome by special techniques such as time-sampling and sampling possible observation posts. Uncertainty can always arise as to whether the observations are representative and as to the identity of the population thought to be represented. These difficulties are not crucial in the exploratory stage but they impose severe limitations when precise data are required about behaviour rather than about the physical and social environment.[12]

If we need information about past events such as how people managed in previous homes, their life history, or their recent activities, then observation is not possible; some form of questioning either in interviews or through questionnaires would be essential. Normally attitudes are difficult to observe, though in a few cases they can be inferred from observable behaviour; for instance from the way in which people react towards tourists, visitors, and coloured people in public, answer their questions or serve them in shops.

Opinions may be seen in letters to newspapers but are not always representative of the general public nor of a particular population. In general, the systematic study of attitudes and opinions would necessitate some questioning.

Notes

[1]Artists often rely on us to add inference to observation when looking at their pictures. Gombrich shows how incomplete visual representations and auditory messages may be interpreted through inferences, sometimes unknowingly. See ch. 7 'Conditions of Illusion' in E.H. Gombrich, *Art and illusion,* Phaidon Press, London, 1962.

[2]B. Russell, *An outline of philosophy,* Allen & Unwin, London, 1927, p. 68.

[3]Michael Argyle, *The social psychology of work,* Penguin, Harmondsworth, 1974, p. 145.

[4]For example, postcards and letters, suitably addressed and stamped, are randomly dropped in an area, or put under car windscreens with a scribbled note saying 'this was found near your car'. The messages on the cards or the addresses on the letters can be varied to cover opposing attitudes; some might be addressed to the Preserve Carlton Campaign, whilst an equal number are addressed to the Develop Carlton Campaign. The different rates at which the two types are duly posted are taken to reflect the attitudes of those who post them. These 'lost letter' techniques and similar ingenious devices are not very efficient.

[5]The observer may be a man or woman. To avoid any suggestion of a restricted sex role, I made several attempts to write this paragraph without using pronouns of any gender. For reasons of style it proved impossible. This shows how language can restrict our thought and modes of expression.

[6]H.J. Gans, *The urban villagers: Group and class in the life of Italian-Americans,* Free Press, New York, 1962; also by the same author *The Levittowners: Ways of life and politics in a new suburban community,* Pantheon Books, New York, 1967. See also W.F. Whyte, *Street corner society: The social structure of an Italian slum,* University of Chicago Press, Chicago, 2nd edn 1955.

[7]J.H. Robb, *Working-class anti-Semite: a psychological study in a London borough,* Tavistock Publications, London, 1954.

[8]L. Festinger, J. Riecken & S. Schachter, *When prophecy fails,* University of Minnesota Press, Minneapolis, 1956.

[9]Gans, *op. cit.,* 1967.

[10]On the use of records see the chapter by Triesman, pp. 295-313, in N. Armistead (ed.) *Reconstructing social psychology,* Penguin, Harmondsworth, 1974.

[11]A.F. Davies & S. Encel, *Australian Society,* Cheshire, Melbourne, 2nd edn, 1970.

[12]I have not mentioned moving observers simply because I have never tried this. F. Yates, (*Sampling methods for censuses and surveys,* Hafner, New York, 3rd edn, 1960) describes a method for counting the number of people in a street or shop. You walk quickly in one direction counting all

the people passed in either direction, including, presumably, those on the other side of the street, but deducting those who overtake you. Returning in the opposite direction at the same speed, you repeat the count. The average of the two counts gives an estimate of the number of people in the street at that time. You could also have two moving observers: they would start at opposite ends and on opposite sides of the same street and compare results.

Further reading

Anyone thinking of participant observation should first read the accounts of those who have used the method successfully. In the second edition of his book, Whyte, 1955, added an appendix on his research methods. Gans, 1962 and 1967, describes the methods and the limitations of participation. The method is also discussed in Denzin, 1970.

Chapter 5

Asking Questions

According to some people, asking questions is just a matter of common sense. For example Moser and Kalton (1971):

> Question designing remains a matter of common sense and experience, and of avoiding known pitfalls. (p. 348)

Common sense by itself is obviously not sufficient, since Moser and Kalton take many pages and examples to describe and illustrate the benefits of experience. The need for rigorous pre-testing advocated by them also indicates that merely relying on common sense could be disastrous. Many chapters and even books have been written giving essential guidance on asking questions and sound advice on the known pitfalls.[1]

These general principles apply whether one is asking questions by mail or in person. An interviewer can sometimes cope with unforeseen difficulties but otherwise the problems are the same. The document on which the questions appear is usually called either a questionnaire, schedule, or guide, according to the method used for obtaining answers.

Questionnaire — for a formal inquiry which the respondent fills in himself. These may be delivered and collected by field workers or through the mail.

Interview schedule or **recording schedule** — for a formal inquiry like a questionnaire, but the interviewer asks the questions and records the answers.

Interview guide — for less formal or even quite informal interviews in which the interviewer may have some freedom to use the most suitable sequence and wording; he also records the answers.

The distinction between the terms 'questionnaire', 'schedule', and 'interview guide' was suggested by Goode and Hatt[2], but has not always been followed consistently by other writers. For convenience I shall use the term 'questionnaire' in this chapter to cover all the above methods unless otherwise specified.

The subject of questionnaire design may refer to the construction of the whole instrument or to the items in it. Questionnaire design as a whole would include selecting the topics or content areas and the general approach to the person selected as respondent; it would also include decisions about the sequence of these topics, the format and layout of the final product, and the manner of carrying out the pre-testing. Design of the questionnaire items refers to the decisions about the exact wording of the questions and the kind of response categories that will be used. I will discuss each of these matters in turn.

Content and approach

The selection of the topics to be included in the questionnaire will depend on what objectives were decided on in the initial planning of the survey. Constant reference to these specific objectives will prevent irrelevance and help to keep the questionnaire down to a reasonable length. Except where special arrangements have been made, an interview should not take more than half an hour. Aim for twenty minutes and the chances are you will finish up just inside half an hour — but only just! A ten-minute interview will be less tiring for all concerned; usually, interview time costs money. If a self-answer questionnaire is too long there will be a lower response rate. Unless there is a good justification for asking about religion or parental occupation, or how much the occupant pays in rates, these items should not be included.

If the questions are too difficult or depend too much on a person's memory, then the accuracy of answers will suffer and also fewer people will respond. With difficult questions special efforts must be made to obtain co-operation, perhaps by explaining the purpose of the items. It should be made possible for someone to admit ignorance without feeling idiotic, rather than being forced to make a wild inaccurate guess or pretending to have an opinion about something he has never heard of before.

The approach to the respondent needs careful consideration. A postal or delivered questionnaire should be accompanied by an explanatory letter asking for co-operation. As far as it is possible to do so without introducing or provoking any bias, the purpose of the inquiry should be explained in straightforward terms. It is never wise or ethical to promise potential benefits from the survey unless there is a reasonable chance that the benefits will in fact result. It is permissible however to say that the results of the survey will:

help (us, the council, etc.) to know more about Collingbourne;

   or,

help the local authority to come to a decision;

   or

give residents a chance to say what they think about certain important issues concerning the locality.

Something to the effect that: 'Your assistance in this important inquiry will therefore be most valuable and greatly appreciated' should always be added.

An interviewer will introduce himself and proceed in a similar manner.

The questionnaire or the letter should state:

1.   the title of the survey (or give some idea of its purpose);
2.   the name of the agency sponsoring the survey; and
3.   (if such is the case) that all or certain of the information is to be treated as strictly confidential.

If it is also an anonymous survey this should be stated. But note that a doorstep interview can hardly be anonymous though it can still be confidential.

In addition, for interviews the questionnaire should have spaces for:

4.   case number;
5.   interviewer's name (or initials or number);
6.   place, date and time of interview.

Classification or identification data — also called profile data

Even if the questionnaire is anonymous there must usually be some information identifying the responses as coming from someone belonging to a certain section of the sample. This classification data may include such items as: name of respondent (or family), if not anonymous; address (again, only if not anonymous); sex and age; marital status; occupation; and educational level.

In addition, in housing surveys you may need to know the relationship of the respondent to the main occupants (for example son, lodger). Many people now regard the term 'family head' or 'head of the household' as offensive. In the United Kingdom census of 1971 two items were regarded as controversial; these asked for 'parents' country of birth' and 'relationship to head of household'. Both items were dropped from the pilot test census in 1974[3].

The wording will need to be thought out carefully. It should not contain jargon such as 'marital status' or 'educational level'. Even a harmless word like 'occupation' can be ambiguous. In the trial runs you must try out such phrases as 'What is your (husband's) job?' Asking people what age they left school can be misleading since many go on to complete further education later. A question such as 'At what age did you finally stop receiving full-time education?' would not give a true picture of the educational level of people who continued with part-time studies. However, it might be useful as an indication of the social class of the respondent's family of origin.

For greater accuracy it is better to ask for date (or year) of birth rather than to ask for age. People often round off their ages and you can get an unrealistic proportion of thirty- and forty-year-olds.

The specific objectives of the survey and the way you intend to group the final data will govern which classification items and other information you will need to obtain.

Two further points must be settled: when and how you ask for the classification data. Usually it is easier to ask these questions at the end because the respondent is no longer worrying what it is all about. He knows the worst! He has not had to divulge deep secrets or be made to feel foolish. Rapport should now be at its best and it should be obvious that the interview is coming to an end. You can then say something like

> Well, those are all the questions I had to ask (about the topic). Your name of course won't be mentioned, but so that we can draw up tables that group similar people together, I would like to ask you a few personal details. Would you mind telling me your date of birth? Are you married now? Were you ever previously married?

There is one exception to the idea of asking these questions last. In quota sampling it is necessary to find out first whether the person fits into the category specified by your quota. Otherwise you could have wasted time if you later found that he was not as young or as unskilled in occupation as you had supposed.

Wording the main questions

In *The Art of Asking Questions*[4] there is a concise check-list of 100 considerations that can be made in the construction of a questionnaire. About a dozen of these refer directly to the words themselves, then fourteen ways are given of avoiding bias or loading, and finally there are nine tips on readability. However, Payne also believes his check-list is mostly 'only common sense' but useful as a reminder.

The following ten rules combine the wisdom or common sense of many writers.

1. Use familiar words, phrases and style.
2. Use simple words and simple straightforward sentences.
3. Be specific — without too much elaborate detail.
4. Ask concise questions that cannot result in ambiguous answers.
5. Be precise and not vague.
6. Keep it short. (Aim for less than twenty words per question.)
7. Avoid bias and leading questions.
8. Do not make presumptions.
9. Be realistic and not hypothetical.
10. Don't make too many rules.

Seriously! The best way of finding out how to ask questions is by trial and triumph, experience and experiment. All questions, especially new or difficult ones, should be pre-tested. Alternative forms of the same items may be tested in a controlled experiment by using the two forms — one for each group — on matched samples or on one sample randomly split into two. More will be said about pre-testing later (pp. 51-2).

The first six rules should ensure that the questions are clearly understood. Rules 7, 8 and 9 are reminders of the importance of avoiding various forms of bias. In other words, these rules can be condensed into two general rules —

1. Be clear. Make sure that you can be understood in the only way you intended.

2. Avoid bias. Make sure that you are being fair. Do not ask questions that may push the answers in one direction.

If you need some illustrations of these points, read on. Otherwise skip the next section.

Familiar words

Though you should always use familiar words it does not follow that a familiar word is necessarily the correct one for your particular question. Use a dictionary, to see if the word has other meanings you had not thought of, and to find alternatives.

Some familiar words and phrases are much too vague, e.g. *'how often?'*, *'how much?'*, and *'how far?'*. It is better (Rule 3) to be specific and ask 'How many times did you have difficulty in parking last week?'

In fact, frequency questions or any others that place too much reliance on respondents' memories should be kept to a minimum. Descriptive phrases like 'often' mean different things to different people.

Distance, say to nearest friend or relative, can be asked for approximately in terms of miles (to nearest ¼ mile) or in terms of time taken to walk, go by car, or public transport. Until people are familiar with the metric scale, it would probably be better to find the location and measure the distance on a map yourself.

Some words change meaning according to context and frame of reference. To a Housing Commission tenant in a multi-storey block, 'other occupants' could refer to members of his own family in the flat, or to other tenants in the block.

Specific terms

Questions should be concrete and specific. 'Do you believe in town planning?' is much too abstract. Terms like regional development, conservation of natural resources, ecological balance, protection of the environment, and decentralisation, are likely to mean different things, or nothing at all, to different people. Most people would probably respond favourably because these are stereotyped concepts. We all want good things, like democracy and protection of the environment. The solution is to indicate specific proposals in words that can be easily understood by the general public. In 1974 the students of Wodonga Technical School in Victoria carried out a survey to find out how the people of the district felt about being in an area planned for accelerated growth. They interviewed 820 people in the district and were surprised to find that they had to explain terms like 'accelerated' and 'acquisition of land' quite frequently.

Ambiguity

Even familiar and simple words can sometimes be ambiguous. 'What kind of house do you live in?' might be answered according to size, structure, age, or style. Asking for reasons (for example, 'Why do you live here?') would produce a range of answers that had no relationship to each other. This is fine in the exploratory stages but here we are concerned with drafting the survey questions. If answers cannot be compared it becomes very difficult to express the data in quantified terms.

Double negatives produce ambiguous answers. What would 'Yes' mean in answer to this question?

> Don't you think we shouldn't turn people out of their homes just to preserve or enlarge a green belt round the city?

The question is too long, and is certainly biased. Note the emotion-arousing phrase 'turn people out of their homes' (instead of 'insist on people moving') and the hidden bias in 'just to' (instead of 'in order to').

Even single negatives can cause ambiguity and bias, as in: 'Don't you agree that it is time for a new town plan?

Bias

There are many ways in which questions give rise to bias. Some have already been mentioned — stereotyped concepts, negatives, and emotional phrases.

Leading questions are obviously biased (just as I am obviously biased against them!) 'Would you say that you are in favour of rent control?' is easier to answer 'yes' than 'no'. A leading or 'loaded' question may sometimes be used to find out how many people are so strongly against a suggested policy that they reject the idea even when the question is biased in its favour. But this is a dangerous game to play and should be left to the experts.

Presuming questions imply something about the respondent that we are not entitled to assume. It is hard for a respondent to deny an assumption. 'How many times a year do you go to church?' may result in exaggerating the number of church-goers.

Hypothetical questions can also produce unreliable information. The answers to 'Would you like to live in a flat?' may be based on frustration.

'Yes' may mean 'anything, even a flat, would be better than this hovel'. Alternatively 'Yes' might indicate a willingness to try anything. In either event, frustration or adventure, no true preference for type of housing can be obtained in this way. Just for fun, imagine how the young rake or the fading roue might respond when the female interviewer innocently asks him: 'Would you like to live in a flat?'

A hypothetical question might get what it deserves — a hypothetical answer. For example:

> Q. 'Would you stay here or live somewhere else if a coloured family moved in next door?'
> A. 'It would depend. If I liked them I might stay. If not . . . .'

Making social predictions on flimsy fantasies should be avoided. Hand the crystal ball over to an expert social scientist.

Bias in the direction of social acceptability or social desirability, that is, respondents giving answers that they believe are more generally approved, can arise if they feel slightly guilty, nervous about their reputation, or wish to create a good impression. Ego-defensive answers can sometimes be avoided by providing suitable face-saving phrases or rationalisations. 'Many people these days have no time for the garden. Did you manage to do any work in the garden last weekend?' Or in a political inquiry: 'In the last election a large number of people were unable to get to the Polling Station. Did you happen to vote?' Look at the extract from *New Society* printed below and try drafting rationalisations

ASKING QUESTIONS WITHOUT AROUSING GUILT!

Industrial firms and unions in Britain have said that resistance from white workers has prevented them from encouraging the employment of more coloured workers. David J. Smith of P.E.P. (Political and Economic Planning) reports:

'We asked the 231 plants which employed the racial minorities, the following question: "Many employers have had a difficult task helping their employees to adjust to the employment of non-white people. When you began taking on non-white people were there any complaints from your white employees?" The introduction to the question was added to make informants feel that it would not be an admission of failure to answer Yes; it ensures that the results do not underestimate the extent of the difficulties encountered.'[5]

to introduce questions on the respondent's own life-style (as distinct from attitudes to other people's behaviour) with regard to attending church, gambling, using the local library, abortion, alcohol and drugs, and keeping dangerous animals.

In permissive societies there are fewer activities about which people may feel defensive. Perhaps permissive-type answers are becoming the socially acceptable norm. Parents may feel constrained to give a young interviewer the impression that, on some matters, they are more permissive than they really are.

Payne can have the last word on words: 'Beware the *double entendre* and shun the triple. "Please check your sex", for example, has three meanings — mark, restrain, and verify.'[6]

Response categories

The method of recording answers needs to be considered when the question is being drafted. In fact the possible range of answers may affect the way you finally decide to ask the question.

In general there are two types of questions and answers:
open or open-ended which permit the respondent to answer in his own way; and closed or restricted to a limited set of response categories, two or more, usually in the form of a check-list. To illustrate the different types, the same items will be asked in both ways. Open questions would be in the form:

1. What do you think of the proposed urban freeway?
2. How do you usually travel to work?
3. Why do you prefer to use the supermarket?

On the printed form, open questions would be followed by a few lines for the answers to be written in either by the respondent or by an interviewer.

Closed questions would be:

1. Do you think they should build
    the proposed urban freeway?   YES   NO
2. Do you usually travel to work
    (a) on foot?   YES   NO
    (b) by bus, tram, train?   YES   NO
    (c) in your own car?   YES   NO
    (d) in a friend's car?   YES   NO
    (e) by other means, if so how? ....
3. Mark (√) the reasons why you prefer to use the supermarket.
    (a) nearer than other shops   □
    (b) cheaper than other shops   □
    (c) more variety than other shops   □
    (d) parking is easy   □
    (e) less walking about   □

Various combinations of boxes or encircling words and numbers can be used.

With closed questions, the answer may be a restricted two-way choice ('yes' or 'no' with usually a third category for 'don't know'), or there may be a restricted multiple choice. Notice that closed questions 2 and 3 are really not true multiple-choice questions since they can be regarded as comprising ten distinct two-way items. But if you ask the respondent to mark only one or two items of the list — 'Which is the way you *most frequently* travel to work?'; 'Which is the *main* reason . . .etc.?', this would be a multiple choice question.

Therefore a series of two-way items may be *less* restrictive and provide more information than a single multiple-choice question. It should be made quite clear whether or not more than one of the possible answers may be used. Sometimes, when more than one answer is permissible, extra information is obtained by an instruction such as: 'Of the reasons you have just marked, put a circle round the box opposite your *most important* reason.'

Other restricted ways of responding include ranking and rating. In **ranking** the items are listed and the respondent is asked to 'put 1 against your first choice, 2 against your second choice', and so on. In **rating** a scale such as

strongly agree	agree	uncertain	disagree	strongly disagree

is used. This would enable a respondent to indicate agreement or disagreement with any given statement or expression of opinion such as: 'More money should be spent on urban freeways.' Or the respondent may be asked how he feels about a whole list of things, and to indicate for each item

very satisfied	satisfied	dissatisfied	very dissatisfied

Notice that in these two examples the positive end of the scale comes first. If this sequence is repeated throughout the questionnaire, it could result in bias due to 'response set' or to the direction of the questions. These points will be taken up later.

Probing and prompting

In interviews, probing for more information is done by first asking the question, recording the answer and then asking for more details. Suitable probes might be

> Why?
> Any other reasons?
> Can you tell me more (about this?) (about your job?)
> Is there anything else?

Prompting is done in two ways: either the list of possible answers is read out by the interviewer, or it is shown to the respondent. In each case this can follow an open question such as

> Which newspapers did you read last week?

After recording the answer or answers, the interviewer follows the instruction to ask the prompt, which could be

> Did you also read anything in any of these newspapers?

Alternatively the prompt can form part of the question in this way:

> Which of these newspapers did you read last week?

and the list is either shown or read to the respondent according to the schedule instructions.

In other words the prompt can be *part* of the question itself, or a *supplementary* question.

And in each case the prompt list can be *read* to the respondent or a prompt card can be *shown* to the respondent. On a printed questionnaire the alternatives are obvious to the respondent so that the list inevitably becomes part of the question, even though it may be printed as a supplementary question.

Pre-coding

Some textbooks give the impression, unfortunately, that the choice is between open and pre-coded questions. This is not the case. Closed or restricted questions are by their nature pre-coded. But in the hands of an interviewer an open question can also be pre-coded. The interviewer asks, for instance,

> What in your opinion is the most urgent improvement needed in Collingbourne?

or

> What are the disadvantages of living in Collingbourne?

and waits for the reply. The possible answers, as shown by preliminary fieldwork, are listed and given code numbers (probably in boxes). The answers are recorded by checking the appropriate codes. If necessary, in order to record which things were mentioned first, the codes or response categories can be numbered in sequence as they are mentioned. In this way a measure of salience or what is uppermost in the minds of the public can be assessed.

Advantages of open questions

Because open questions permit greater freedom of expression, they help the interview to sound like an ordinary conversation. This puts the respondent at ease, starts him thinking and talking about the topic. For these reasons interviews often begin with an open question such as

> What do you think of this town as a place to live in?

Open questions encourage a richness and depth in answering and this is essential in the preliminary fieldwork. But because of the resulting greater variety, with a larger sample and team of interviewers in the survey, the interpretation and allocation to pre-coded categories often becomes extremely difficult. Statistical treatment and comparisons may be impossible.

Not all people respond to open questions with a flow of information. Some become tongue-tied, suffer from mental blocks or feel awkward. Perhaps this is because an open, unstructured question provides no guidelines as to what kind of information is expected.

Check-lists[7]

Check-lists can be used to suggest a wide range of possible answers. They indicate the appropriate frame of reference and help the respondent to think of other possibilities. This may sound like gentle coercion, and indeed an interviewer may unknowingly put stress or a pleasant intonation on some items if he has to read out the list. However the check-list can be handed to the respondent with a question such as

> Did you decide to move to this district for any of the reasons given on this card? If so, which?

Check-lists are meant as reminders and not as arm-twisters.

Only comparable items should be included. The instructions should say if only one or all items may be checked. Usually, as in political elections, the first item will receive 2 or 3 per cent more mentions just because it is first. Items can be rotated to avoid this effect.

An interviewer must be instructed whether he is to read out the list to the respondent; show the list to the respondent; or use the list solely for the purpose of recording answers.

To maintain a standardised procedure all interviewers must receive and follow the same instructions — on this matter as on everything else. However, these instructions may require the interviewer to show the list to the respondent but permit the interviewer to read out the list in special cases. When this is done, the fact must be recorded and the reason (illiteracy, poor sight) given.

The 'don't know' problem

Inevitably some answers will fall into that misty area between 'yes' and 'no', or between 'agree' and 'disagree'. These are put into the 'don't know' category even though they may be due to a variety of reasons.

Interview failure

The question was not heard or understood properly. The interviewer did not hear the answer or did not wait long enough for a reply. Perhaps the respondent hesitated — 'Well, I don't know . , ,' (down goes the answer) . . .'Yes, I suppose I would' — but it is too late: the interviewer is already looking at or even asking the next question.

Ignorance or lack of information

1. Information was not available; 2. information was available but was either not seen or not understood.

For example: 'Do you think the Government should go ahead with its housing scheme?' Preliminary questions will help to sort out those who have not heard about the scheme or who have not yet had time to consider it.

Indecision

Having considered the matter the respondent can come to no definite opinion either way. This is a genuine point of view and you should allow for this.

Indifference

They have heard about it but do not feel they need bother themselves with the problem.

A series of questions preceding the opinion item could follow this form:

(a) Have you heard of the X scheme?
(b) Have you had time to consider it?
(c) Do you think it matters much whether the scheme goes ahead or not?
(d) Do you think the scheme should go ahead?

After a negative answer to either (a) or (b) there is no need to proceed with the rest.

Sequence of the questions

As we shall see later, one of the advantages that interviews have is that a standardised procedure can be followed in all the interviews. For one thing the interviewer controls the sequence of the questions whereas with self-administered questionnaires there is very little control over this factor. The respondent can look ahead to see what is coming. For both methods there are some general guidelines.

The introduction, whether written or spoken, must create interest and motivate the respondent to co-operate and to respond sincerely and accurately. The purposes of the survey should be given broadly and the sponsorship stated.

The first few questions should be interesting and simple, thus assuring the respondent that he is going to be neither bored nor floored. Early items should not require something that reflects unfavourably on some people, such as items indicating level of education or social and economic status. This would create resistance.

As far as possible follow the natural or psychological order. To avoid sudden jumps from one topic to another, insert suitable bridging passages.

Sticky questions should come in the body of the interview, about or just after midway, when rapport is strongest and before boredom or impatience sets in.

It should not be possible for answers to be influenced by previous questions. If a respondent is forced to take a stand on one issue, it is much harder or even impossible for him to modify his position later when other questions suggest different possibilities or require different sorts of comparisons. Once a train of thought has been narrowed to a particular aspect, it becomes difficult to put this in proper perspective when broader issues are involved. This early focusing may result in bias.

For example, in one survey it was necessary to find out to what extent people would be worried if they thought they had cancer or other diseases. We also wanted to know if they were aware of the possible signs of cancer. Therefore the first part of the interview did not focus on cancer. Instead, we asked general questions such as 'Which disease would worry you most if you thought you had it?', and 'Which disease do most people die from in this country?' After this there were a few questions in which cancer was mentioned, along with six other diseases, on a prompt card. About a dozen questions later there was a short bridging section:

> There has been a lot in the papers about cancer lately. Could you give me your views on some aspects of it? What do you think could be the first signs of cancer?

Now obviously, if we had asked questions about cancer first, then the two general questions just quoted about disease would have brought in extra references to cancer. This would have produced a form of positive bias, due to premature focusing, which we were anxious to avoid. For the same reason it was necessary to use interviews rather than postal questionnaires in order to control the sequence of questions.

Response set

Another form of bias that can be avoided to some extent is that resulting from response set. The respondent may automatically agree or disagree without properly considering each item. Persistent agreement is more common than disagreement and is termed the **acquiescent** or **agreement response set.** Those people who would do anything for a quiet life are probably more prone to agree than others. There is evidence that some personality tests have been contaminated with response set.[8] If there is a sequence of questions in which agreement indicates satisfaction (in other words, the questions are all in the same direction), then there could be a positive bias in the results and a risk of exaggerating the degree of satisfaction among respondents. This is partly avoided by mixing the sequence so that 'Yes' sometimes indicates satisfaction and sometimes dissatisfaction. It is better, obviously, to do this in a randomly counterbalanced manner using a roughly equal number of positive and negative items, instead of merely alternating them. (See the extract from the *Australian Psychologist* reprinted opposite.)

Theoretically you could avoid sequence effects by randomising the order and the direction of the questions.[10] This could be done when the form is designed so that all subjects receive the same (and therefore standardised) random sequence. Alternatively, you could randomise the questions over the whole survey sample so that a number of different random sequences would be used. Both methods are liable to upset the logical sequence of the questions. But the desirability of randomising questions should always be considered, if only to bring to light any possible in-built sequence bias.

Of course, some people are determined to be 'agreeable', highly satisfied, or perceived in a favourable light, so if they can, they will try to answer 'correctly' (i.e., yes or no, depending on which answer indicates satisfaction or agreement with the respectable point of view). This, once again, is the intractable problem of social acceptability or social desirability.

ATTITUDES TOWARD THE ROLE OF WOMEN IN SOCIETY[9]

You are asked to express your feelings about each statement by indicating whether you (A) agree strongly, (B) agree mildly, (C) disagree mildly, or (D) disagree strongly.

a few of the items are given below

1. Swearing is more repulsive in the speech of a woman than of a man.
2. Women should take a more active part in solving the social problems of the day.
3. Women being drunk is worse than men being drunk.
4. Sons in a family should be urged to go to university more than daughters should be.
5. Now that many women work outside the home men should share in household tasks such as washing dishes and doing the laundry.
6. It is insulting to women to promise to obey their husbands in the marriage service.
7. A woman should be as free as a man to propose marriage.
8. Women should worry less about their rights and more about becoming good wives and mothers

The scale is scored in the direction of women's equality; a low total score on the whole scale of 25 items would indicate a conservative attitude. Thus "agree strongly" with items 1, 3, 4, 8 would score zero and "agree strongly" with the positive items 2, 5, 6, 7 would score 3 for each item.

You might like to consider whether a scale like this would be affected by
  (a) social desirability bias, and
  (b) response set bias.
What advantage, if any, is there in having a mixture of positive and negative items?

Format

If the questionnaire is to be left with members of the public, it is worth while presenting a well-printed form on reasonably good quality paper. A cheap-looking, amateurish, duplicated questionnaire does not inspire confidence in the authenticity and competence of the survey sponsors. The layout will depend on whether questions are open (allowing lined spaces for replies) or closed (with appropriate boxes for replies).

Much will also depend on whether the data are to be punched on to computer cards. For computer purposes the following important points must be borne in mind.

(a) The columns on a computer card allow for ten categories or codes, numbers 0 to 9. Normally there should not be more than a choice of one out of nine possible answers for any one item, leaving at least one code for 'no data'. If you require more than one for 'no data' (e.g., 'no reply' or 'item missed'; 'not applicable'; 'don't know'), the number of permissible answer choices for the item must be reduced accordingly. In most cases eight or nine response categories will be enough; if more are needed, then it is possible with some computer programs to include letters of the alphabet as well as the numbers. Make sure first that the program you intend to use can cope with alpha-numeric tabulations.

(b) You may not need all the 80 columns on a computer card but the ones you do use should all be punched once. Even if there are no data you must punch the appropriate 'no data' code (usually 0 or 9). Unpunched columns can cause problems in tabulation.

(c) Each column in use should be punched once *and only once*. Depending on the program, the computer will usually terminate your program if multi-punched columns are detected. So if multiple responses are allowed for any question (for example, 'Check any of the following items that you usually buy locally') you will need a column for each item or response category. You must consult a programmer if you are likely to have more than one column for any question.

(d) Make sure that your questionnaire records all the details that you are likely to require in analysis. Response categories can always be collapsed into larger groupings later. For example the different Protestant churches can each be given a separate code and you can decide later to classify them all as 'Protestant'. But if you include only one code for Protestants on your questionnaire it is obviously impossible to break this up into different varieties later. Categories can be numerous at first and collapsed later; the reverse procedure is not possible.

On all of these points it is advisable to consult a computer programmer before you finally draft the questionnaire. Do not wait until you have printed the form. This may seem like putting the cart before the horse; as yet you have no data to program. However, it is wise to make sure that any available horse will be strong enough before you load your cart. You must avoid producing an impossible coding system.

The completed questionnaires must be coded in such a way that the card puncher can run through them at a maximum speed. If you expect a card puncher to use the 'hunt and peck' method which is used by most untrained typists, you will produce confusion. This will result in errors and missed items. If possible the coded items should appear in the correct sequence down the right-hand side of each page.

Usually you or your assistants will do the coding with the aid of a coding manual which you will have constructed for this purpose. However it is possible for an interviewer, or reasonably literate respondents, to do this at the time of answering. You need first a general instruction, such as: 'Please record your answers in the boxes in the right-hand column'. Then each item must give a code, like this:

Single	Married	Separated or Divorced	Widow or Widower
1	2	3	4	

Another system is to have the respondent or interviewer mark the appropriate square with a special pencil. A 'mark sensor' machine can then be used: this will 'read' the forms for computer purposes; it also enables the cards to be punched if necessary. Problems can arise if there is more than one page to read.

In some questionnaires it will be necessary to use **filter items.** For example:

Q.25 Do you drive a motor vehicle?   YES   NO

If 'YES' answer questions 26-30;
If 'NO' answer questions 31-35. | 1 | 2 | |

We should always remember that some respondents find it much easier to indicate their replies by circling the answer or marking a box with a cross; they might find numbers confusing and their writing may be hard to decipher.

Pre-testing

This is a simple matter which is often omitted. The purpose is to check the suitability of the wording and of the range of answers provided (and hence the coding). It can be done in two ways. First by trying the questions on experts, colleagues, friends and acquaintances. This may in fact be sufficient, but if you can, also try the questions on a small sample of people who are similar to those in your survey population.[11] In any event, try to avoid using people who may later be part of your survey sample.

A more rigorous test will come in the Pilot Survey but meanwhile many errors can be avoided by a little pre-testing on, say, ten to twenty people.

Another form of pre-testing is to imagine what your data will look like when you get replies. By drawing up dummy tables, relating one item to another, you can see whether your proposed questions will give you the required information. It is probably a good idea to guess what numbers might go into your tables: this might lead to splitting large categories into sub-categories in order to make a finer analysis possible — if the problem so requires.

If your mock tables seem complete without using the information from questions on, say, religion or car-ownership, then you should seriously consider dropping those items.

Notes

[1] Books with advice on how to ask questions include: C.F. Cannell & R.L. Kahn, ch. 15 in G. Lindzey & E. Aronson (eds), *The handbook of social psychology, vol. 2: Research methods,* Addison-Wesley, Reading, Mass., 1968; W.J. Goode & P.K. Hatt, *Methods in social research,* McGraw-Hill, New York, 1952, ch. 11; Moser & Kalton, *op. cit.,* ch. 13; Oppenheim, *op. cit.;* and S.L. Payne, *The art of asking questions,* Princeton University Press, 1951.

[2] Goode & Hatt, *op. cit.,* p. 133.

[3] *New Society,* 25 April 1974, p. 176.

[4] Payne, *op. cit.,* pp. 228-37.

[5] *New Society,* 20 June 1974, p. 696.

[6] Payne, *op. cit.,* p. 234.

[7] A comparison of open and check-list items is reported in W.A. Belson & J.A. Duncan, 'A comparison of the check list and the open response questioning systems', *Applied Statistics,* vol. 11, 1962, pp. 120-32. (Also published as Reprint Series No. 29. The Reprint Series publishes many reports about specific problems regarding the method of asking questions which have been investigated by the Survey Research Centre, formerly of the London School of Economics.)

[8] There is persuasive though not conclusive evidence that some standard measures of authoritarian personality, including the famous F scale (F for Fascism), are seriously affected by acquiescent response set. All items are positive so that agreement increases the score in the authoritarian direction. See A. Hughes, *Psychology and the political experience,* Cambridge University Press, 1975, ch. 4 'Problems and solutions in measuring psychological dispositions'.

[9] Taken from G. Stanley, M. Boots & C. Johnson, 'Some Australian data on the short version of the Attitudes to Women Scale (AWS)', *Australian Psychologist,* vol. 10, no. 3, 1975, pp. 319-23.

[10]The direction of a question can be a problem when one alternative must be presented before another in the same question. An example would be 'Do you approve or disapprove of the Government's policy on conservation of open spaces?' This problem also applies to rating scales. Belson, 1966, found that the negative end of a rating scale received more support when it was presented first instead of last. (See W.A. Belson, 'The effects of reversing the presentation order of verbal rating scales', *Journal of Advertising Research,* vol. 6, no. 4, 1966. Reprint Series No. 37.)

[11]A systematic method of pre-testing is described in W.A. Belson, 'Respondent understanding of survey questions', *Polls,* vol. 3, no. 4, 1968. Reprint Series No. 40.

Further reading

There is an easy introduction to 'Questionnaire construction and interview procedure' in Selltiz *et al.*, 1960, pp. 574-87; this provides a convenient bridge to the next chapter on interviews.

Chapter 6
Interviews

Wordsworth must have been a very poor interviewer. In his poem *Resolution and Independence* he describes how, one morning after a stormy night as he was walking across the splashy moors, he met a leech-gatherer. This is how he began the interview (lines 82-84) —

> And now a stranger's privilege I took;
> And, drawing to his side, to him did say,
> 'This morning gives us promise of a glorious day.'

—a rather starchy opening which must have made him sound like a bishop. Nevertheless —

> A gentle answer did the old man make,
> In courteous speech which forth he slowly drew:
> And him with further words I thus bespake,
> 'What occupation do you there pursue?
> This is a lonesome place for one like you.'
>
> (lines 85-89)

Wordsworth goes from bad to worse. This is not the way to ask how a man makes his living. And in any case before the old man has a chance to reply, Wordsworth puts ideas into his head which might influence his attitude towards his environment. 'This is a lonesome place for one like you'.

The old man describes his 'occupation' at great length but before long Wordsworth is not even listening.

> But now his voice to me was like a stream
> Scarce heard; nor word from word could I divide;
>
> (lines 107-108)

One of the worst faults in an interviewer is not paying attention and forgetting to listen carefully to everything that is being said.

Wordsworth recovers his presence of mind and renews his mission —

> ... My former thoughts returned: (113)
> My question eagerly did I renew,
> 'How is it that you live, and what is it you do?' (118-119)

That's better! Wordsworth has reworded his question to suit the respondent — in words of one syllable. Compare his first attempt above in line 88.

This example illustrates what we might call 'the tender approach'. But Lewis Carroll, poking fun at Wordsworth, gives his own version in *Through the Looking Glass* as follows —

> I cried, 'Come, tell me how you live!'
> And thumped him on the head.

With all its faults, I would prefer Wordsworth's tender approach to this tough style of interview.

There are *tough* or stress interviews in which pressure is applied to a person in order to extract a confession; and there are *tender* interviews of the counselling or clinical kind which are intended to help the person being interviewed. These are not the terms usually applied to interviews in social surveys where the style of interviewing can vary from very formal to very informal. A very formal interview may seem relatively tough in its rigidity and lack of opportunity for self-expression; a very informal interview is flexible and certainly more like a helpful interview with plenty of opportunity for self-expression and therefore relatively tender. But this is about as far as the comparison can be stretched.

In this chapter the different styles or types of social survey interviews will be described using the formal-informal distinction; the merits of the two styles will be compared. The main advantage of formal interviews is seen in the claim that they achieve greater standardisation and therefore produce more reliable quantifiable data. This claim will be examined. At every stage from obtaining an interview to reporting the responses it is possible to maintain a high level of standardisation, but only if the method is thoroughly understood and appropriate procedures are followed. The purpose of this chapter is to show how the best results can be obtained from the different styles of interviews.

Types of interviews

A **formal interview** is one that follows a set form. The questions to be asked are all decided before the interview; the exact wording is used in each interview and the sequence of questions is strictly controlled. Except for planned randomisation or rotation of items the sequence is the same for each interview. So there are set questions asked in a set sequence. Most of the questions are of the restricted answer type though a few open questions might be included. In any case the answers are recorded according to pre-coded categories in a standardised form.

A very formal interview, highly systematic and standardised, is like giving a questionnaire verbally and is quite unlike a natural conversation.

Interviews may be much less formal than this or even quite informal depending on the survey design. The interviewer proceeds as the situation requires, asks the questions in any convenient order and may explain questions or even change the wording if necessary. Sometimes he may add extra questions. None of these variations would be permitted in a standardised, formal interview.

In very **informal interviewing** there may be no set questions but just a number of topics that are raised at appropriate moments. This would come closest to an ordinary conversation but since it would still be 'a conversation with a purpose' it would fall within Kahn and Cannell's definition of an interview.[1]

Many other terms are used to indicate this difference between formal and informal interviews. Here are a few.

Types of interviews

FORMAL	INFORMAL
structured	unstructured
systematic	unsystematic
controlled	uncontrolled
standardised	qualitative
extensive	intensive
guided	unguided

Clearly there can be gradations of formality to informality; that is, the differences form a continuum and not a dichotomy. Some interviews may be a mixture of two types, beginning in an informal style and finishing more formally (or vice versa). Notice that 'informal' refers to the method and not the setting. You could have an informal interview in the manager's office or a formal interview in the cottage parlour.

With these considerations in mind, a few examples will be given of different types ranging from very informal to formal.

Typical of the unsystematic interview is that of the employer who asks the first question that comes into his head when selecting staff; or the tourist as he rubber-necks his way around the city.

On a more scientific level but still very informal would be the casual conversations described by Zweig that 'were not formal interviews but an exchange of views on life, labour and poverty'[2]. Zweig found that these friendly, casual talks with working-class men were more fruitful than questionnaires or formal interviews.

A very special style of informal interview leaves the direction of the conversation in the hands of the subject without much guidance from the interviewer. These 'unguided' interviews were probably first used in social research by Elton Mayo in the pioneering Hawthorne investigations[3]. About the same time Carl Rogers was using a similar 'non-directive' technique which he made famous and used to good effect in his 'client-centred therapy'[4]. The idea is to keep the respondent (client) talking and following out his own thoughts without external direction. The interviewer proceeds with a series of encouraging grunts and 'A-ha's', brief sympathetic comments ('That must have upset you'), and encouragement to continue ('Tell me more about what you feel about . . .'). Probing to find out more clearly what the respondent thinks is also done by reflection and by summary. The interviewer acts like a mirror (reflection) and repeats or 'echoes' the respondent's last phrase: this starts the respondent talking again. At suitable points the interviewer briefly summarises what the respondent has just said and this leads to further elaboration or possibly modification and correction — but the respondent keeps on talking! There are no set questions and usually no predetermined framework for recording answers. In fact taking notes in long-hand becomes almost impossible because of the concentration needed in listening. A tape-recorder becomes essential. (See p. 63 regarding the advisability and the ethics of using tape-recorders.)

There is no doubt that on suitable occasions the non-directive style can be very penetrating. The method avoids imposing any hypothesis or any assumption about the existence of an attitude. Whatever is of importance to the respondent is what *he* chooses to talk about and this gives us a method of assessing saliency. Since the subjects are able to get things off their chests in this permissive atmosphere they often feel better for the interview. But it is a time-consuming business and when Mayo changed from guided to unguided interviews, the average interview time trebled from half an hour to 1½ hours.

Another disadvantage of unguided interviews is that the respondent may never spontaneously reach the topic most central to the research project. When I participated in a study of the electrical engineering industry in England, we began with unguided interviews and found that the foremen talked about everything connected with their work — everything, that is, except the one thing that interested us most, namely the methods of supervision they used. Consequently we had to change to a guided type of interview in which we asked them specific questions about their contacts with their subordinates[5].

The strictly unguided, non-directive Rogerian technique requires great skill but you can explore the possibilities of the method on a number of social occasions — at a party for instance. See how long you can keep the other person talking before you are forced into stating an opinion or giving away any information yourself. Of course if you run into someone who is doing the same thing, conversation will quickly grind to a halt. There are limits to the number of times two people can say 'A-ha!' to each other.

Another type of interviewing that moves further in the formal direction is the funnel approach or what we might call 'gently guided' approach. At first, a broad, general question is asked, such as: 'What do you think could be done to improve this district?' This is followed by successively more restricted questions until gradually the content of the conversation is narrowed to precise objectives. 'Do you approve or disapprove of the proposal to reserve Heathmont Heights as a public golf course?'

This sequence prevents early questions from conditioning or biasing later responses. It also uncovers the respondent's frame of reference, his personal and social criteria, and his value system, before pinpointing a local issue. Once again saliency can be assessed from the thoughts that seem uppermost in the early part of the interview. The golf course may not even get a spontaneous mention.

The procedure can be inverted — we turn the funnel upside-down. The inverted funnel approach begins with one or more specific questions and then goes through a number of sub-areas. Finally an overall assessment is obtained — 'Now taking all these things into consideration, what do you think of this town as a place to live in?' Or 'Could you now tell me what is the most important thing that needs to be done here?' This ensures that a wide view is taken of all the relevant aspects of the situation before passing judgment. Otherwise a recent incident, such as the rare failure of the local bus to run that morning, could produce warped opinions.

Another 'gently guided' approach, which is similar in many ways to the two just described, is the **focused interview.** As an initial stimulus a suitable topic is chosen as a focus. This might be a news item or a local event or issue. After providing a focus (perhaps more than one) the interview becomes non-directive. People will stay close to or move away from this focus according to their prominent interests.

In a study of Australian farmers, questionnaires were used as a basis for focused interviewing . . . 'to let conversations develop naturally and to ask particular questions when a given topic had come up'[6]. Thus questions were not completed in the same sequence, which was not important. But additional material was obtained which was used for content analysis to obtain a cross check.

In general, the 'gently guided' approach method provides the flexibility of informal interviewing but gives the interviews a framework and ensures that all relevant topics are discussed. Usually there is no set questionnaire and most of the questions are open ones. Respondents are thus not restricted in their replies and the interviewer does have some freedom. Though not completely standardised, they are systematic to the extent of getting relevant information by using definite headings covering specific areas.

At the formal end of the scale is the **firmly guided interview,** completely standardised and systematic — as was said earlier, just like giving a questionnaire verbally. For reasons that are discussed later, this is the kind of interview used most widely in opinion polls of all kinds and in large sample surveys.

Figure 1 shows the increasing degree of formality of the different types. One other type of interview can be used in social surveys. The **group or** 'snowball' interview is mainly used in market research, especially the motivation research variety. It involves a recorded discussion between four or five people all of whom have a common interest, such as buying newspapers. Newspapers from different countries may be piled on a central table and selected by members of the group, inspected, and passed round. The 'interviewer' becomes more of a discussion leader whose job is mainly to listen, give everybody a chance to say something, and to prompt occasionally. Suitable freely-worded questions may be brought in to the discussion at intervals.

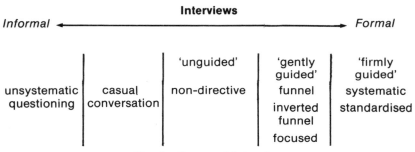

Fig. 1   Types of Interviews

In my experience this is rather like enriched systematic observation and is therefore a method of discovery more than a method of proof. But there is no reason why this method cannot be used as part of the preliminary work preceding a social survey.

Choice of interview method

The extent to which the interview should be formal or informal will depend upon the purpose of the research, the stage or phase in the survey plan, the time available for interviewing, and the skill of the interviewer.

Informal methods are essential in the preliminary explorations. They are likely to be more comprehensive, cover a wider range, and go deeper into the individual's attitudes and feelings. In this way one can hope to clarify the problem, find out what the important issues are, and suggest relevant hypotheses.

But informal interviewing requires greater skill on the part of the interviewer. It also requires deeper knowledge of the subject matter and the vocabulary involved. To some extent the knowledge and vocabulary can be obtained in preliminary discussions and training. Maintaining a relevant conversation without unduly restricting or interrupting the respondent is a skill that comes from considerable clinical training or from extensive training and fieldwork. Unless a team of highly skilled interviewers is available, informal interviewing is not suitable for large-scale surveys.

Informal interviews are more liable to interviewer bias. The interviewer partly determines the trend of the interview, the questions that are asked, and the details that are recorded; his report may have 'more of the interviewer' in it than would a questionnaire. Consequently, different interviewers will obtain different results and the reliability (consistency between interviewers) is less than with formal interviews. Generally speaking, what is not very reliable cannot have high validity (i.e. truth). If two interviewers produce different results, how can we tell which, if any, is the real answer?

However it is claimed that when deep emotions are involved, informal methods may produce data closer to the truth. People answer more truthfully in a friendly, informal interview that gives them full scope to express themselves. In one such interview a woman described how she once felt a lump in her breast but did not think at the time that it might be cancer. Later in the interview she referred to the same incident and exclaimed with some feeling '. . . and *immediately* I was afraid I might have cancer.'

In favour of formal interviews it is claimed that the snap answer to a snap question may be more valid than one carefully thought out after a long discussion, especially when the question involves social attitudes. People will respond quickly to support an opinion that demands the suppression of pornography or an unpopular political viewpoint, without realising that this is not consistent with the notion of freedom of the press. People may be genuinely angry about the activities of a local industry polluting the river and express their opinion before considering the implications for local employment or for 'free enterprise'.

Arguments about the statistical treatment of the results can also be used to support both formal and informal methods. In favour of formal methods it is claimed that without standardisation: you cannot compare different items of information; the answers from questions worded differently are not truly comparable; and statistical analysis is difficult.

Against this it can be said that a more complete picture of a person's attitude is obtained through flexible informal interviewing, and this is lost when it is compressed into statistical tables.

To each according to his taste, as Whistler said when he threw a pot of paint in the public's face and caught Ruskin's eye[7].

The relative merits of the contrasting types can be summed up as follows:

Informal interviews: are richer in detail, and go deeper; provide finer discriminations; and are more qualitative.

Formal interviews: have greater uniformity because they are standardised; therefore provide greater comparability of data; allow for more sophisticated statistical treatment; are more quantitative; can cover a greater sample; are quicker; are less expensive; are less vulnerable to interviewer bias and inconsistency; give less room for interviewer error; and hence have higher reliability.

Standardisation

Clearly everything depends on the claim that formal interviews provide for greater standardisation. If this claim is false then all the alleged advantages listed above collapse like a row of dominoes. In that case we would be claiming more for formal data than is justified, without being aware of the weakness of our method. Much better, then, to use highly skilled interviewers informally and treat the results with caution than to rely on the false security of formal data.

Though complete standardisation is never possible with informal methods, there are some precautions that may be observed in any form of interviewing. These will now be discussed.

Obtaining an interview

Except in quota sampling, the interviewer does not choose a subject. The person to be approached will be nominated by the sampling procedure. The method of approach and the wording of the opening remarks form an essential part of the instructions to all the interviewers. They should all give exactly the same information regarding the sponsors and purposes of the survey and there should be a standard reply to any request for further information. All interviewers should carry identification cards which they must show when they introduce themselves. Wearing a label or badge can be too conspicuous.

Some interviewers may feel that any refusal to be interviewed is a failure on their part and that extra pressure to get a volunteer, by stressing possible social benefits from the survey, or by other comments, is justified if they can keep the refusal rate down to a minimum. This introduces an unwanted variability in the type of volunteer.

The survey policy on maintaining the anonymity of respondents or the confidential treatment of all information must be stated clearly in a standardised form. If the respondent wants to know why he was selected, a standard reply should be given.

To maintain a standard approach the introduction should be as brief as possible so that it can be memorised accurately. In the first minute or two the interviewer should be looking at the respondent and not staring down at a piece of paper.

If any interview is not obtained the reason must be recorded and there should be instructions covering when (for example, that evening, next day) and how often the interviewer must call back to make renewed attempts.

Probes, prompts, and persistence

An interviewer should not try to reduce the number of 'Don't know' responses by repeating the question unnecessarily, by expressions or exclamations of surprise or other forms of persistence. Of course, if it was a simple factual question such as 'Do you travel to work by train?', a polite repetition should be standard procedure.

There should also be a general instruction to cover responses that do not convey a clear meaning or that are not properly heard. For example:

> I'm sorry, I don't quite understand that. Could you say a little more about it?
> I'm sorry, I didn't quite hear that. Could you say that again?

In no circumstances should the interviewer attempt to guess what was meant or said. This increases the chance of bias or else of just straight error as was demonstrated in an experiment by Smith and Hyman reported in Hyman et al.[8]

It should not be left to the interviewer to decide when and how to probe for further information or to prompt by indicating possible replies. The occasions and the phrases should be printed on the interview form; the use of prompt cards was described in Chapter 5.

In formal interviews, probing, like other open questions, is kept to a minimum: 'Could you tell me more about that?', 'Why do you think that?' But in informal interviewing a skilled interviewer can use a variety of probing devices with the effect of bringing out new information or correcting previous responses[9].

Recording responses

Few interviewers can write clearly when they are trying to keep pace with someone talking. This leads to mistakes in coding back at the office. Even a few slightly indistinct words can cause coding errors. Therefore it is wise to restrict actual writing to a minimum and have responses recorded by crosses or ticks and strokes through the appropriate boxes. Since we are conditioned to thinking that a cross means an error, perhaps a respondent should not see us entering crosses for his answers!

Immediate coding can save much time later but only if the interviewer can write figures clearly and unambiguously. It is surprising how many hurried note-takers can make 5 look like 6 or even 8. Alterations must be absolutely forbidden; the wrong entry must be crossed through with an X and the correct entry made in the space just to the right of the box.

Alternatively, the code numbers may be printed across the page after each question (and below the response categories) and the interviewer rings the appropriate number. This prevents errors due to poor figure writing but slows down the card-punching process. The use of a special mark-sensor pencil could rectify this.

Standardisation of recording is most difficult with informal interviews. Some open questions can be pre-coded but making notes while the person is still talking is a tricky business. When I interviewed Broken Hill miners underground, we made notes for about an hour per interview, using our helmet lamps. Later in the day, we would read back our notes, using a tape-recorder, and elaborating wherever it was reasonable to suppose our memories were accurate. Under these conditions it was possible for each interviewer to complete only four interviews a day (two before and two after lunch) either underground or on the surface.

Interviewers vary, both in the amount that they can write during an interview and in their interpretations and summarising of lengthy discussions. This is one reason why informal interviews are less reliable. Tape-recording can overcome this to some extent but should never be attempted without the respondent's consent. This would be an infringement of the ethical code. Some people may be slightly put off by seeing the tape-recorder and this could reduce their spontaneity. On the other hand, the conspicuous notebook may have similar effects. Hughes[10] describes one of his subjects in an interview: 'Noticing the interviewer writing in long-hand, he slows his remarks to dictation pace.' A speaker who slows down could introduce extra time for self-censorship. Though a respondent can see that you are taking notes, it is always courteous to request permission. This can be done on the grounds of greater accuracy or 'because I shall be seeing over a hundred people during this survey'.

Closing the interview

There is not much room for unreliability here, but a few standard instructions will ensure a smooth finish and a maximum of usable information.

Before departing, the interviewer *must* make sure that all the questions have been asked and all responses recorded. He will feel awkward doing this while the respondent sits or even stands waiting and may in his haste fail to notice gaps. There are two ways of overcoming this:

1. *Say* 'That seems to be about all, thank you. But while I make sure that I haven't missed anything perhaps you might like to think about anything you'd like to add or to ask me.'

The other method was one I introduced when there were more than a hundred items to be checked:

2. *Say* 'That seems to be about all, thank you. But while I make sure that I haven't missed anything, perhaps you would not mind answering the questions on this piece of paper.'

A two-page questionnaire, mostly multiple choice items and a few write-in items, was then handed to the respondent with a pencil. This could finally be checked at a glance.

The interview is clearly brought to an end by putting away the papers, asking if there is anything else the respondent wants to say, and thanking him for his help.

Sometimes, when the planned interview is firmly closed the conversation free-wheels in a very rewarding manner. I have known a works manager tell me more about management's decision processes after the interview, as he conducted me through the factory to my next assignment, than it was possible to elicit during the actual interview. In another survey, a woman said during the interview that cancer patients should be treated in general wards along with other patients. After the interview, in an emotional outburst, she said quite the opposite and demanded their complete separation. There is evidently much to be gained from an 'ostensibly-closing-the-interview' technique.

After departure and before beginning the next interview, notes must be made of impressions regarding the respondent's attitude during the interview. Descriptive notes should be added of the person's characteristics, his home or work-place; details must be given of any particular difficulties encountered during the interview.

Instructions

It will now be obvious that to ensure standardisation, clear instructions must be given to all interviewers regarding every step from obtaining an interview to ending one. General instructions should be printed and explained in briefing sessions; interviewers should be asked to refer to their copies frequently.

Instructions contained in the body of the questionnaire should be printed in capitals. Use lower-case print for everything that the interviewer has to read out.

No variation or modification of the instructions can be allowed with formal interviews. This should be clearly understood by all concerned. However with informal interviews there may be some latitude, and the points and extent where this is allowed should be emphasised.

The Interviewers' Manual should remind interviewers of the general rules covering interviewing, such as: reading out questions clearly; proceeding at a suitable pace; listening carefully; and not interrupting. It can also cover such matters as appropriate dress, wearing badges, and so on. Drawing attention to these details helps to emphasise the need for standardisation in everything that might otherwise influence someone to give a biased reply. The research director should explain this and not run the risk of being ignored as a fussy authoritarian conservative. In response to such explanation my students have when necessary worn their best (or only) suit, sought official permission to discard clerical garb or clothes of their religious orders, and even had hair-cuts in order to present a neutral appearance when interviewing.

Training

Untrained staff are one of the chief causes of unreliability in interviewing. Experiments show that untrained interviewers are less successful in obtaining interviews, and that training decreases the percentage of total entries that have been omitted or are unusable.

Interview training can be a very lengthy business. The United Kingdom Government's Social Survey training program involves up to three weeks of initial training followed by three to six months of probationary work in the field. Other courses vary from five to twenty hours, rather than weeks. The optimum training period, taking into account a cost-benefit analysis, is not easy to estimate. My own experience is that students who have spent at least four hours rehearsing the actual questionnaire that they are going to use in the survey, can perform at a very high level of efficiency.

After lectures and laboratory sessions (another four hours in all) on the principles of interviewing, the students study the actual questionnaire in detail. Then, in groups of four, A interviews B whilst observed by C and D. The interview is tape-recorded (but video-tape would be better). Then the observers give their comments and the 'respondent', B, gives his reactions and impressions. The recording is played back to illustrate these points and bring out others. Then the roles rotate until each student has been interviewed once, acted as interviewer once, and been an observer twice. They quickly notice their own mistakes and help each other. By using a central observation room between two interview rooms, a trained interviewer-tutor can supervise two such training groups concurrently.

A few students require a second session. Otherwise the next step is to carry out three or four interviews on friends and relatives until a word-perfect performance is possible. Because the actual questionnaire is used for training, the interviewers are more likely to become familiar with the wording, and less variable.

A small band of people who are keenly interested in the social survey, trained specifically on the actual survey material, firmly convinced of the need for objectivity, scientific accuracy, and the use of standardised procedures, is better than a host of semi-professionals who are anxious to get the job over. The other possibility is to use hundreds of experienced but occasional interviewers in the hope that their errors and biases will cancel out. But to that end the interviewers should be randomly selected and randomly assigned to random samples.

Survey supervision

The final link in the chain to ensure standardisation of procedure and high reliability of results is good supervision. This is needed in the training of interviewers and during the period of the survey fieldwork. If the research director does not have trained staff available for this purpose, then he will have to supervise the interviewers himself.

A central survey office is needed, where interviewers can call in or telephone whenever queries or difficulties are encountered. Preferably at the end of the first morning, or at the end of the day, interviewers should bring in their completed questionnaires for checking. This enables the supervisor to ensure that instructions are being followed right from the start of the survey. The supervisor should check such things as: understanding and following of instructions; clarity of writing and coding; accuracy of coding; response rate — any special difficulties in obtaining interviews; and item completion — frequency of missed items and 'Don't know' responses.

Even if the interviewer has reached a high level of performance, it is still advisable to have all work brought in daily. This ensures a steady flow of work for checking and card-punching and so on, and lowers the risk of completed questionnaires being lost and going astray.

Some fieldwork checks should be carried out if possible. The supervisor can spend some time with each interviewer (especially new ones) observing their procedure and manner, improving their performance if necessary.

This still leaves open the possibility of faked returns or false claims to have carried out interviews that in fact never took place. Some follow-up checks are necessary, either by post or by telephone or in person. A postal check is of limited value since it is usually restricted to asking only a small proportion of the questionnaire items with the main purpose of finding out whether the person was in fact interviewed. If people are asked to indicate the fact that they were not interviewed, by making a cross for example, the chances are that people who have been interviewed are more likely to return the card or form than those who have not been interviewed. Those who were interviewed have, presumably, no more worries; but the others may fear that by revealing the fact that they were missed out they might get someone into trouble, or get a full length questionnaire, or have an interviewer call on them. So why bother to answer the inquiry?

The postcard method of verifying personal interviews in a survey was tested in an experiment by Hauck[11]. A thank-you letter was sent with a postcard asking a few questions about the interview to each of 587 people who had been interviewed and to 580 who had not. Of those who had been interviewed, nearly half returned their postcards; 2 per cent of these postcards reported that there had been no interview. Of those not interviewed only 9.5 per cent or one in ten returned postcards, and of these, 15 per cent incorrectly reported that they had been interviewed. As Hauck says, whatever the reason, 'the important fact is that people who have not been interviewed cannot be relied upon to return a verification postcard.' Those who do are not necessarily representative of the survey population.

'Older respondents were more likely to return postcards than younger ones' and the better-educated more likely than those with less education. The postcard method of interview verification is therefore a poor form of quality control on surveys. Though the telephone or personal contact methods may take longer and be more expensive, they are more likely to detect falsified interviews and provide more reliable information.

The usefulness of the telephone as a means of verifying interviews depends on how many of the survey population have a telephone. There is also the problem of bringing the right person to answer the telephone. A follow-up visit is probably the best method unless the respondents belong to a special category or profession.

A personal call by a supervisor means that a respondent can be re-interviewed, ideally without knowledge of the previous responses (i.e. a 'blind' re-interview). In this way the two sets of responses can be compared. With a sufficient number of re-interviews a measure or estimate of reliability can be obtained. The only problem is how to get a respondent to answer the same questions again. Some ingenuity is required. The supervisor might say 'Some interviewers are better than others. We would like to see how good our staff is in this survey.'

It is only necessary to re-interview about 10 per cent. If the interviewers know in advance that one in ten of their respondents will be followed up in some way, either by a re-interview or in a second stage of the survey, they are unlikely to run the risk of faking returns or missing out interviews. They should also be given some feedback on the quality of their interviewing, say, the percentage of items on which the supervisor obtained identical answers.

Re-interviews are not possible if the survey is anonymous. This is a good reason for having a 'confidential' survey with a guarantee that the names of respondents will not be known outside the office.

Notes

[1]R.L. Kahn & C.F. Cannell, *The dynamics of interviewing: theory, technique and cases,* Wiley, New York, 1957, p. 97.

[2]F. Zweig, *Labour, life and poverty,* Gollancz, London, 1948, p.1.

[3]F.J. Roethlisberger & W.J. Dickson, *Management and the worker: an account of a research program conducted by the Western Electric Company, Hawthorne Works, Chicago,* Harvard University Press, Cambridge, Mass., 1939.

[4]C.R. Rogers, 'The nondirective method as a technique for social research', *American Journal of Sociology,* vol. 50, 1945, pp. 279-83.

[5]M. Argyle, G. Gardner & F. Cioffi, 'The measurement of supervisory methods', *Human Relations,* vol. 10, 1957, pp. 295-313.

[6]F.E. Emery, & O.A. Oeser, *Information, decision and action,* Melbourne University Press, 1958, p.vii.

[7] *Pace* Gombrich! (E.H. Gombrich, *The story of art,* Phaidon, London, 8th edn, 1957, p. 401).

[8] H.H. Hyman, W.J. Cobb, J.J. Feldman, C.W. Hart & C.H. Stember, *Interviewing in social research,* University of Chicago Press, 1954.

[9] For examples of the way this can be done see Goode & Hatt, *op. cit.,* pp. 194-206.

[10] Hughes *op. cit.,* p. 82.

[11] M. Hauck, 'Is survey postcard verification effective?' *Public Opinion Quarterly,* vol. 33, 1969, pp. 117-20.

Further reading

The authors who have written most about the art of interviewing are probably C.F. Cannell and R.L. Kahn. See their chapter 8 'The collection of data by interviewing' in Festinger & Katz, 1953; also their chapter 15 'Interviewing' in Lindzey & Aronson, 1968, vol. 2; and Kahn & Cannell, 1957. These books should be sampled and used for reference when necessary; some repetition is inevitable.

Manuals for interviewers include J. Atkinson, 1967; and Survey Research Center, University of Michigan, 1969.

For focused interviewing see R.K. Merton & P.L. Kendall, 'The focused interview' pp. 476-89 in Lazarsfeld & Rosenberg, 1955.

For group interviewing see Scott, 1952. Appendix B (pp. 177-84) gives a balanced summary of the advantages and disadvantages of group discussion as a research technique.

Chapter 7

Choosing the Survey Method

The customer is not always right. Survey clients often suggest the wrong problem and select the wrong method. Just because you are asked to draw up a questionnaire to distribute to geriatric patients does not mean that you should go ahead without considering other possibilities. Perhaps a fairly free-flowing informal interview might be more appropriate, depending on the nature of the problem.

Practical considerations such as the feasibility of observation and the availability of trained interviewers must, of course, always be taken into account. But they should not be allowed to dominate the decision regarding choice of method. A ready-made questionnaire or a team of interviewers standing by with nothing to do, may be helpful. On the other hand, methodological principles demand that the most appropriate methods and instruments should always be selected; only in special circumstances should something available be allowed to dominate decisions about the survey design.

Often the main choice of method for collecting quantifiable data will be between interviews (of one type or another) and self-administered questionnaires. For the purpose of this comparison 'questionnaires' will refer to those questionnaires that have to be completed by the respondent ('self-administered') and returned by mail or collected. Interviews, except where otherwise stated, will refer to all types. The essential difference then is the presence or absence of an interviewer when the questions are being answered.

Before comparing the relative advantages of the two methods, we should consider the possible effects of using an interviewer.

In an interview there are two sources of human error — the interviewer and the respondent. The interviewer may read out the question incorrectly or in such a way that some answers are more likely than others. The respondent may hear the question incorrectly or may answer incorrectly either through carelessness or deliberately through wishing to deceive or impress the interviewer or to avoid censure. Without knowing it, the respondent may be influenced by subtle cues given by voice and dress which suggest the social standing of the interviewer. In accepting the answer, the interviewer may screen out unwanted information or hear incorrectly. Whether the answer is heard correctly or not it may be recorded incorrectly; for instance the interviewer may use the wrong code of may write down only part of the answer.

All of these errors, whether mainly due to the interviewer or the respondent or to the influence of one upon the other, are known as **response errors.** The response that is recorded does not exactly correspond to the one that was given or one that would most nearly represent the truth.

Response errors may be of two kinds. If they are due to carelessness or inattention they will be more or less random; they may even cancel out over the survey as a whole as when the number of people who insincerely state or are incorrectly recorded as favouring a planning proposal are counterbalanced by the people who appear to oppose it when in fact they are in favour. A repetition of the survey, closely resembling the first one and using the same sample, would produce the same overall result, though many individual responses would appear to have changed. Individual response variations could be pooled and averaged and this would give the response variance for the survey population. This is only possible if the same errors are not recorded for the same individuals on each occasion; in other words the errors are not systematic, they are random.

But they may not be. The errors recorded by one interviewer or by a group of interviewers may go consistently in one direction rather than another. This is the other type of response error that is the result not of random carelessness but of bias; the errors are systematic. The extent of the bias will not be revealed if the survey is repeated unless the nature of the bias is known and can be counterbalanced for instance, by using different interviewers.

Bias is a persistent problem in interviewing. Notice that an interviewer has two or three chances of making a mistake. It might look as if a questionnaire is less vulnerable; the respondent can read the question more than once and can take as long as he likes to think about it. This may, of course, result in falsification, though it should reduce the number of careless errors. Theoretically, only one source of human error is involved if we ignore for the moment the possibility of any coding errors made by the office staff. With two people involved it would seem that the interview is twice as likely to produce errors. But this is an oversimplification of the comparison. Many of the errors that are possible in an interview are also possible with a questionnaire; but a good interviewer can prevent many errors that might otherwise be made by the respondent on his own.

Response errors resulting from interaction between interviewer and respondent

Interview bias, in the broad sense, refers to any systematic errors, consistently leaning to one side, that arise from the interaction between interviewer and respondent. This includes all systematic response errors from either source and from any cause in the interview. Within this general category, interviewer opinion bias refers to systematic error due to the opinions of the interviewer.

Opinions of interviewers

Common sense would suggest that if an interviewer has strong opinions regarding the issue being investigated, results will be biased in the same direction. A few studies have demonstrated this very clearly[1]. It is possible that the interviewer's opinions do not have to be particularly strong for this effect to occur. In a study on opinions towards prefabricated houses the results reflected the interviewers' own opinions for and against prefabricated houses. In market research there is a tendency known as the 'sympathy effect'; interviewers are inclined to produce results that exaggerate the popularity of their employer's products.

By using interviewers with known and contrasting views the results can be weighted or biases can be balanced so that they cancel out and produce a picture that is reasonably accurate for the total sample. Balancing biases for small sub-groups within the sample might be very intricate or even impossible.

Obtaining an interview team with balanced biases may not be easy. Because interviewers tend to come from a narrow population stratum it is likely that their biases will go in the same direction. Most interviewers are middle class and share a similar educational and occupational background; their age differences are small. Consequently, on many social issues they will share remarkably similar views. For example, in England concern for the environment appears to be mainly a middle-class attitude, at least according to Goodchild[2]. In a study based on a sample of fifty residents of Market Drayton, he found some clear differences. Compared with the working class in that area, the middle class put greater stress on aesthetic improvements; have a stronger preference for living in attractive surroundings; and tend to attach greater significance to local buildings with historical interest or high architectural quality.

The interviewer's own opinions about issues covered in the interview do not always influence the results. Respondents are likely to resist any obvious bias and may even resent it, but they might find subtle bias difficult to detect. Cantril[3] found that on matters where people were uncertain they could be influenced by interviewer bias 'but where opinion was well crystallised, biasing statements had relatively little effect on the results.' Interview training is directed towards the elimination of all forms of bias; well-trained interviewers are not likely to communicate their own views to respondents.

Hyman and his team made a special study of interview bias and have shown that the interviewer's own opinions affected responses only under unusual circumstances; with exceptionally difficult questions and with respondents of the same social class as themselves, interviewers tended to detect their own views in the respondents. Perhaps this was projection.[4]

However, there is no reason to be complacent about this. Open questions are particularly vulnerable to interviewer bias. Shapiro[5] employed about forty interviewers to obtain data on voting intentions and four different criteria for choosing how to vote; a random sample of 215 registered voters in the State of Hawaii was selected for the research. Analysis of the results revealed an unexpected interviewer bias factor. Shapiro thought some interviewers (despite their instructions) might have pressed their respondents harder on each of the open questions so that more items were mentioned; other interviewers were less forceful and recorded fewer items. In a separate study, Collins[6] has shown that interviewers not only vary in the amount they record but also have distinctive personal verbal preferences when recording answers to open items. Collins suggests that this could result in bias. It is easy to see that the encouraging nods and smiles of an interviewer may influence the choice of words and the length of the answer; and that the longer the answer the more chance there is that views similar to those of the interviewer will be mentioned and receive approval.

To summarise this section, we may say that interviewer bias is more likely to occur

1.   when the respondent's opinions are not fully crystallised;
2.   when the interviewers are not well trained, or depart from their instructions;
3.   when questions are difficult or ambiguous;
4.   when interviewer and respondent belong to the same social class;
5.   with open items rather than the restricted answer type.

Personal characteristics of interviewers

Interviewers vary in ways that are immediately obvious to the respondents; sex, age, race, and personal attractiveness are quickly assessed by the respondent — though probably not consciously. In the first few moments of introduction the respondent will also notice such things as personal appearance, style of dress and speech; these will indicate the interviewer's level of education and social class. I sometimes suspect that this preliminary assessment diverts attention from the interviewer's carefully phrased explanation of the purposes of the survey.

This preliminary assessment, as well as the explanation of the survey, affects the respondent's reaction to being asked to answer a few questions. A respondent agrees to be interviewed partly to please the interviewer; agreement indicates a willingness to co-operate and be helpful. Anyone who has no desire to please the interviewer and sees no reason for co-operating, can usually find an excuse for refusing to take part in the survey. But a willing respondent wants to do the right thing and please the interviewer; what psychologists call 'the demand characteristics of the situation' operate. In seeking or accepting an invitation to 'come inside and sit down while we talk', the interviewer increases the possibility that the respondent will want to please and impress him. Social norms demand that we treat guests with respect, try to please them, and not antagonise them with unwelcome opinions. Whether inside the house or on the door-step, most respondents are likely to say, if they can, what they think the interviewer would like to hear; to avoid any possibility of antagonism, respondents may find it difficult 'to tell it the way it is'.

This form of interview bias has been particularly noticeable with racial characteristics. Interviewers who appear to be Jewish, whether they are Jewish-looking or introduce themselves by Jewish names, receive fewer anti-Semitic responses. During the Second World War, Negroes in a southern U.S.A. city were asked by white interviewers 'Do you think it is more important to concentrate on beating the Axis or to make democracy work better here at home?'; 62 per cent replied 'beat the Axis.' Of an equivalent sample interviewed by Negroes, 39 per cent replied 'beat the Axis'. Speaking to white interviewers, Negroes under-reported their education and car ownership; in these and other matters Negroes presented a relatively passive view of their expectations. This was less noticeable in New York.

Times may have changed and the rise of black consciousness, increased open mistrust of whites, and public hostility towards them should decrease Negro reticence when speaking to whites. But even in 1960, Negroes in southern rural areas showed larger response differences according to the race of the interviewer than were found among Negroes in southern urban areas. Clearly these effects 'require continued study as race relations themselves change'[7].

The perceived social class of the interviewer appears to influence the respondent to give replies thought to be acceptable to that class. For many years election forecasts tended to underestimate support for labour parties. This was due to labour supporters being unwilling to express their true views to middle-class interviewers. How do we know that this was not another example of interviewer opinion bias? Firstly, because in matters concerning political parties it is relatively easy to measure and balance bias due to the opinions of the interviewers; secondly, in public opinion polls of this kind open questions are clearly pre-coded and no interpretation of the response is necessary before marking the appropriate code.

If you want to get to the heart of working-class attitudes it helps if you are working class yourself. However, there is an advantage in being an outsider from another country.

> A complete outsider can usually be more easily accepted. He does not fit so well into preconceived patterns; even if he is middle class he is not obviously the same as the middle classes to which the working class is accustomed.[8]

and so the outsider's attitudes would be a mystery to the working-class respondent. Robb also believed that his temporary status was an added advantage. In England social class differences are easily recognised by speech accents which not even a change of clothes will disguise. But English people generally and Londoners especially find it hard to identify the social class of Australians and New Zealanders by their speech. No doubt James Robb of New Zealand also found this was an advantage when he made his study of working class attitudes in Bethnal Green in the East End of London.[9]

Expectations of interviewers

Against a background of street noises, the mumbled answer must somehow be coded. Many other difficulties may arise for the interviewer who is anxious to get something down and not to miss out any items. What does an interviewer do when the long and involved answer does not fit neatly into any of the pre-coded categories? Or if the answer is short and uninformative? Perhaps the reply does not seem to answer the question or else it falls right between two of the categories provided. Some of these difficulties occur in mail questionnaires, as many of us have discovered when trying to fill one in truthfully. Inadequate coding should have been remedied by pre-testing but it can still present difficulties for the interviewer. And no amount of pre-testing or interview training will eliminate the barely audible answer.

Instructions to the interviewers should cover all these eventualities. But sometimes the interviewer is tired or forgetful or in a hurry. The chances are that the interviewer will guess. Without realising it we make these guesses on the basis of our expectations as to what is possible or probable. We assume, for instance, that people are consistent, though alert interviewers soon learn that this is not true of all people. After a respondent has expressed his views in the early stages of an interview we think we can predict how he will answer the remaining questions. Sometimes we are right but there is always the possibility that someone who appears at first to be quite radical will later give a more traditional answer; the true blue conservative may have views on some points that do not fit this description.

Evidence shows that difficult or vaguely heard answers are likely to be recorded in a manner that is consistent with previous answers. Is this bias or random error? Since the error is in the direction of exaggerating the consistency of response patterns, it is a form of bias.

This also applies to another form of expectation based on role. As interviewers we may have our expectations as to which members of the family work in the kitchen or buy the food, who pays the rent, takes the children to school, and who paints the house. There are some interviewers who still expect to find that women lack social consciousness and are only interested in social problems that directly relate to the family. These sex role expectations are being shaken by women's liberation movements but other role expectations remain deeply entrenched; for example, those based on occupation and age. In a society that aims at removing any form of discrimination in employment, old age can still be a barrier, regardless of individual ability.

THE MISSING QUESTION

8(a) Do you have a television set in your home?

Yes 1

No 2

Don't know 3

0

8(b) On how many evenings have you watched television in the last 7 days? (*Ring number stated.*)

1	2	3	4
5	6	7	0
Don't know	Y		

Despite instructions to ask question 8(b) of *all* respondents, a few interviewers asked it only if the previous answer was 'Yes' to 8(a). In all other cases they coded 'zero' to 8(b) *without even asking.*[10]

Social acceptability

Pride may produce bias towards answers that are socially acceptable. People may overstate how often they go to church, borrow books from the local library, visit aged relatives, and in general do the kinds of things expected of a good citizen. Other activities and interests might be understated because the respondent believes the interviewer would disapprove of them. People like to give a good impression of themselves and may slant their answers in order to appear respectable.

Though the response error is made by the respondent, it is another case of interview bias due to the way in which the respondent reacts to the interviewer. There are ways of reducing this bias. Special attention must be given to the wording of sensitive items. They should be asked at a point in the interview where rapport and confidence may be highest. It might be necessary to consider intensive and repeated interviewing of a small sample.

Some surveys have made deliberate use of bias by directive interviewing. The Kinsey research team asked questions about various forms of sexual activity and put the onus of denial on the respondents; their interviewers always began by asking *when* respondents first engaged in such activity. More recently this method was used in an experimental research that was conducted in order to find ways of studying the highly controversial topic of illegal abortions in the USA[11]. Just over two hundred women between the ages of 35 and 50 were interviewed. Half of them were asked a number of non-directive questions such as: 'Did you ever have an induced abortion or do anything to stop a pregnancy?' The other half were asked similar questions in a directive form, in this case: 'When did you have your first abortion or do something to stop a pregnancy?' However, the form of questioning made no difference to the overall results, though some women were influenced by the type of question. Previously it had been thought that less educated respondents would be more suggestible but in this study it was the better educated women who responded more frankly to directive interviewing.

How does the interviewer unwittingly influence the respondent? Clothes, speech, and mannerisms may indicate the social class of the interviewer and the respondent may slant his replies to fit in with the views thought to be appropriate to that class. In the American-Italian slum pubs of Boston, Gans[12] bravely tried to converse with men on their own terms; however he could not bring himself to pepper his speech with sufficient four-letter obscenities and was obviously not accepted; he had to be content with listening and with close observation. It is difficult for an interviewer to avoid giving any clues that might suggest a favourable attitude to some opinions and not others; the respondent may quite unknowingly pick up these clues and follow their leads in reply. A poker face may give nothing away but how can an interviewer behave in a friendly or even normal manner and at the same time present a neutral poker face? Murmurs of appreciation, smiles and nods, as well as positive and negative grunts have all been shown to have influential effects upon respondents.

A hesitant respondent might be prompted by an interviewer who is anxious to obtain full answers; alternatives might be suggested which might not otherwise have occurred to the respondent. If this departs from the standard instructions there will be the danger of bias — which will probably lean in the direction of the interviewer's own opinions. Listening to a more talkative respondent, an interviewer will tend to select those words and phrases that seem 'right' and this will produce a similar bias. As we saw earlier, problems about prompting, probing, and recording are all more likely to occur with open questions, but even restricted questions can be affected by previous gestures and vocal noises.

Some of the response errors described in this chapter apply to questionnaires also, but the absence of an interviewer does not remove all bias, and other errors are likely to arise. If, from the same respondent, different interviewers or different questionnaires obtain different answers to the same questions, **reliability** is said to be low. Reliability is a measure of the consistency of repeated measurements (or assessment of opinion, and so on) under comparable conditions. If the answers, whether consistent or not, do not reflect the true state of affairs, then **validity** is low. Validity is the veracity or truthfulness of the data compared to acceptable criteria.

In the next section we shall consider systematically the relative advantages and disadvantages of the two methods of asking questions and the extent to which reliability and validity may be claimed for them.

Advantages of interviews

1. *More personal*

The interviewer can answer questions about the purpose and sponsorship of the survey (providing his replies are standardised): he can also generate rapport.

Replies can be more candid, since the respondent does not have to commit himself in writing. However, sometimes a more impersonal situation seems to encourage greater candour. In one study, questionnaires brought out more adverse comment about supervisors than did interviews. Similarly, in another study more unfavourable attitudes were found in results from questionnaire than from factory interviews.

Complex, emotional topics can be handled by skilled interviewers. Even extremely delicate aspects of sexual behaviour have been covered in surveys using interviews. Kinsey in the USA probably succeeded with interviews where questionnaires would have failed: the interview study of illegal abortion has already been mentioned[13]. In Britain, Schofield has interviewed young people about their sexual behaviour and also interviewed homosexuals and marijuana or 'pot' smokers[14].

Finer discriminations of response are possible.

People usually enjoy being interviewed and may even feel better as a result of having someone to talk to.

Appreciation can be shown to the respondent.

2. *More qualitative information*

Emotional, hesitant, and excited reactions can be noted. The interviewer can distinguish between a genuine and an insincere response, a serious, thoughtful reply and an attempt to be funny.

Straight-from-the-heart reactions can be aroused. Ostentatiously closing the interview may bring out off-the-record comments.

Observation of behaviour is sometimes possible during an interview: relations with other members of the family (children, old folk) and the use made of various parts of the house (for example, using the kitchen for meals); reactions to subordinates and managers at work.

Observation of surroundings can be useful for social classification and may in some cases be related to the main purpose of the survey (for example housing conditions, state of building, need for repairs, and so on).

3. *Interviews are more flexible, less restrictive*

An interviewer can give an unprompted question (i.e. an open question without suggested responses) and follow this with a prompt if necessary.

He can also probe for reasons etc. and follow up leads (see p. 44).

In an interview it is easier to use filter items in order to omit blocks of questions (see below).

A FILTER ITEM

'If unmarried and over 35, skip to question 40, page 6; if unmarried and under 35, answer questions 30-35; if married, answer questions 30-40.'

An interviewer can cope with this. But in a printed questionnaire these filter items could cause trouble for some respondents.[15]

One advantage of using interviews is that questions can be put in a variety of ways instead of being printed in a questionnaire. Techniques such as paired comparisons (offering a choice between two alternatives, in a sequence that repeats items coupled in various ways) can be used in questionnaires or interviews. But card sorting, and using photographs or pictorial illustrations as the material for questions can best be handled by interviewers.

4. *Greater motivation and ease of response*

This is partly due to the personal factor in interviews which allows for more explanation and builds up rapport (see p. 77).   In addition —

People find it easier to talk than to write, and therefore probably prefer being interviewed to filling in a questionnaire and accordingly, give more information. But in one study, Stouffer *et al.*[16] found that more detailed free comments were written down by the men themselves in the self-administered forms than were recorded by the interviewers. In this case, the subjects were American soldiers who were soon to be released from army service, and they were seated in groups in classrooms during duty hours. This 'captive audience' situation, with the added incentive to keep on writing which would result from being in the presence of others who were doing the same thing (the 'social facilitation' effect), does not apply to individuals who receive a questionnaire through the mail. Incidentally, the same study found that lesser educated men were less articulate in both situations — interviews and the classroom.

Interviews are essential with illiterates; and are preferable for less intelligent or less educated respondents and with foreign-speaking ones.

5. *Interviews yield more complete data*

Trained interviewers can obtain a very high response rate, almost 100 per cent of the sample. In the three years, 1969-71, my students achieved response rates of 98 (twice) and 96 per cent on samples ranging from 508 to 660. Interviews are the only way of ensuring a truly random sample. Mail questionnaires seldom achieve response rates greater than 50 per cent unless the subject matter is of direct interest to the recipients or their level of education is higher than average. However sponsorship is also important and the Government Social Survey in the United Kingdom has obtained rates of around 90 per cent from mail inquiries.[17]

An interviewer can sense if all questions are being understood and can reword or repeat some questions (if his instructions permit this) to improve their chance of being clearly understood.

An interviewer can ensure that all questions are asked and that answers or some entries are made for all items.

Interviews can be repeated as a check on reliability.

Follow-up procedures, and re-questioning sub-samples for further information, though not restricted to interviews are probably easier with interviews.

6. *Standard procedure and control*

Interviewers can control the sequence of the items; the respondent cannot look ahead and anticipate the trend of the inquiries.

Interviewers can control the situation and circumstances of answering the questions — who answers, whether unaided by others, and where.

7. *Interviews can be more valid*

It follows that opinions may be more valid because the respondent must answer immediately and has no time to consult others; the responses should therefore reflect more accurately the respondent's own views.

8. *Preliminary exploration*

Interviews are essential in the exploratory stages of a survey — to discover issues and generate questions.

These are some of the main advantages of interviews but it must be remembered that some of these benefits may be gained at the expense of standardisation and reliability. For example there is opportunity for the interviewer to depart from his script when giving additional explanations about the survey, explaining questions, probing and prompting. Flexibility is one of the great virtues of the interview but in the final, quantitative survey, flexibility must not be allowed to get out of hand. If this happens, then there is no hope of retaining comparability of results from different interviewers or even from one interviewer's respondents: systematic quantitative analysis would then become very risky.

With this in mind, here are some other warnings.

Disadvantages of interviews

1. *Reliability*

As just explained, this could be low, especially for the more informal type of interview. Even with very formal interviews reliability can be lower than for questionnaires because the presence of an interviewer can produce response error and bias.

2. *Validity*

Validity is affected by reliability and cannot be high if reliability is low.

Interviews are not usually anonymous, except when obtained in the street or market. At least the person's address is known when house calls are made. The respondent may not be completely convinced about the confidential nature of the survey.

At least one person, the interviewer, is going to hear the replies. The respondent may therefore give respectable answers rather than honest opinions and statements of fact.

Some loss of validity may be due to interviewer error. Of course this can also happen when a respondent is filling out a questionnaire but then he can at least see what he has written; he cannot usually see what the interviewer puts down. If interviewer errors are random then they may cancel out and still produce valid results for the sample as a whole but possibly not for sub-sections within the sample.

But these errors are likely to produce bias, either intentionally or unconsciously.

The possibility of interviewer bias effects can throw doubt upon the validity of the results. These effects are not solely due to the interviewer's own bias, which may or may not be present, and can often be kept under control. The interviewer's characteristics and social class may influence the respondent to react in a particular way to 'please' the interviewer.

In defence of interviews, high validity can be claimed for election polling forecasts, especially now that better sampling techniques are used and the tendency of middle-class interviewers to obtain underestimates of labour party supporters has been overcome. (See page 82.)

Higher validity than for other methods has also been claimed, but not proved, for intensive interviews. These can uncover deep-seated emotional attitudes such as racial prejudice and authoritarian tendencies, especially when depth probing and projective techniques are used.

3.   Cost

Interviews are relatively expensive for a sample of a given size. The cost factor may limit the survey to a smaller sample, even if interviewers are unpaid.

Interviews take time — and space — if home calls and street interviews are not suitable.

Travelling time and expenses may be involved.

Interview time may cost the respondent's employer money or lost production. In special circumstances it may be necessary to pay respondents for their time.

Training interviewers take time and can add to the cost.

The work is very tiring. Time should be allowed between interviews for note-taking, travelling, and obtaining the next subject.

4.   Difficulty of recording

The problem of taking full notes of a conversation during an interview is usually solved by restricting writing to marks or numbers. But the difficulty still remains especially for informal interviews.

AUSTRALIAN FEDERAL ELECTIONS — MAY 1974
HOUSE OF REPRESENTATIVES

Opinion Polls 11 May 1974
Elections 18 May 1974

Parties   Opinion Polls (Percentages)[18]

	ANOP	ASRB	McNair-Anderson	Morgan Gallup	Actual Results
ALP	50	51	52	49	49.3
L-CP	45	43	43	46	45.8
AP	3	2	3	3	2.3
DLP	1	3	1	1	1.4
Others	1	1	1	1	1.2
Total	100	100	100	100	100.0

KEY
Polls:

ANOP   Australian National Opinion Polls

ASRB   Australian Sales Research Bureau

McNair-Anderson (published in newspapers as the 'Gallup Poll')

Morgan Gallup (which claims that it is the only Australian member of Gallup International)

Parties: ALP   Australian Labor Party

L-CP   Liberal Party-Country Party (Coalition)

AP   Australia Party

DLP   Democratic Labor Party

The advantages of mail questionnaires

To some extent these advantages only reflect the disadvantages of interviews.

1. *Less personal*

The personal factor was given as one of the merits of interviewing, but in favour of questionnaires there are two counter-claims: they do not need rapport; and questionnaires can be anonymous — but not if identification is required for follow-up studies or for cross-tabulating (i.e. for comparison) against other variables.

2. *Standard procedure and control*

Better standardisation of wording can be obtained by using the printed instead of spoken word. No subtle voice inflections, word emphasis, or change of words can affect the impact of the questions.

Printing the available response categories makes for more precision in replies and makes scoring easier and more exact. This may be at the expense of subtle discriminations that an interviewer could pick up.

The respondent fills in his own answers and so cannot be misheard.

Better standardisation means higher reliability and makes more sophisticated statistical treatment possible (for example, scaling).

3. *Absence of bias.*

With no interviewer present, there are no interviewer error or bias effects (except any that might be produced by the respondent's interpretation of the sponsorship).

The respondent is free from any pressure of being observed.

4. *Cost*

Questionnaires are more economical and provide larger samples for lower total costs.

They are less time-consuming (but may take longer to prepare and test) and do not involve travel.

No training of interviewers is required.

Questionnaires can be given in groups (at school, for instance) providing there is ample space to avoid overlooking.

5. *More convenient to respondent*

He can fill in the questionnaire in his own preferred time.

Where factual information is required (family history, illnesses, statistics, number of employees, accidents at work or driving) the respondent can refer to records.

Disadvantages of questionnaires

These have all been stated or implied in the previous sections though new or more detailed points are made here regarding the incomplete sample resulting from questionnaires. The other points are brought together here for easy reference when considering whether or not to use questionnaires.

1. *Incomplete Sample*

The low response rate from questionnaires is notorious; it ranges from 15-50 per cent as against 70-98 per cent for interviews. This poor return can be improved by having collectors call back, more than once if necessary, until time runs out.

As a result of the low response rate the sample is biased. It is no longer a random sample as intended but a sample of self-selected volunteers. These will usually be people who are interested, better educated, of higher socio-economic status, and, of course, those who have more leisure. Busy housewives with children will certainly be under-represented.

In some other important ways the sample will be disproportionate, depending on the nature of the survey population.

2. *Incomplete and inaccurate data*

Items are often omitted; replies to open questions may be vague or illegible. (Of course, these problems may occur with careless interviewers also, but are more likely with self-administered questionnaires.)

Questions and instructions on method of answering may be misunderstood — but not if properly pre-tested.

Few people have the patience or the motivation to write as fully as they would speak.

Complex instructions (for example, 'filter' items) may be confusing.

3. *Questionnaires lack qualitative depth*

Replies may be careless or random, especially if questions are not understood or the matter is not taken seriously.

Replies may be guarded and not spontaneous. But would an interviewer fare any better?

Questionnaires usually offer fixed alternative answers; these may unduly restrict the choice of the most appropriate response. On the other hand, to use open questions depends on a high degree of literacy.

4. *Lack of control, some loss of standardisation*

Arguments about which method provides the most control and standardisation of procedure swing back and forth depending on which type of interview is being compared with mail questionnaires. Normally, questionnaires can reach a high level of standardisation, but there are three aspects that need watching.

The respondent may depart from the printed sequence.

There is no control over the situation in which the questionnaire is completed.

There is very little control over who answers the questions or whether another person 'helps' or influences the respondent.

If the effects of these are likely to be important, then safeguards must be attempted or else interviews must be used.

5. *Inflexibility*

This can be an advantage since inflexibility may reduce unwanted variability in the procedure. But it has its drawbacks.

Once the questions have been sent out, no further explanation is possible. Pre-testing should have eliminated any ambiguities or difficulties.

Probing is awkward, or even impossible.

Are questionnaires any good?

It is obvious by now that I am biased. Other things being equal I would advocate the use of interviews whenever possible. And yet questionnaires clearly have many advantages and have been used with good results. Typically this method is used when taking a population census, for example. True, the questions are usually simple and factual; moreover there is a collector (or enumerator) to help if any difficulties arise.

With social surveys that go beyond the demographic information required in a census, there are circumstances in which it is actually better to use questionnaires rather than personal interviews. These are —

When distance is a problem. If respondents live a considerable distance away or they are widely scattered, a mail questionnaire would save time and the expense of travel. Surveys of university graduates, for instance. When Political and Economic Planning (PEP) in Britain conducted a survey of 2000 women graduates, a useful response of 55 per cent was obtained.

When the respondents are 'busy people'. There are many kinds of people with long and varied working hours whose time is precious, such as working wives, mothers of growing families. Some of them might prefer to talk to an interviewer during a tea-break or over lunch, or when the children are in bed, rather than complete an impersonal questionnaire. Others, like doctors and some university lecturers trying to write in their spare time, might resent any interruption. They would probably prefer to answer questionnaires when it is most convenient to them; and they should have no difficulty in understanding the printed word.

In 1953, questionnaires about cancer education were sent to all

General Practitioners in Britain. Only 24 per cent replied — 2370 for and 2683 against cancer education[19]. If opinions about the National Health Service had been sought, the response may well have been greater. When questionnaires relate directly to a profession, and the survey is conducted or sponsored by a high prestige group, high response rates can be expected. In the United Kingdom the Working Party on Midwives obtained a response of 81 per cent in a pilot survey of midwives. The Nuffield Research Unit at the University of London Institute of Education received a response of over 80 per cent from mail questionnaires sent to teachers[20].

When accurate information is required rather than opinions. This would be the case when details of household expenditure are required. It might be necessary for records to be kept over several weeks in order to cover fluctuations. In industry, factory managers and personnel staff may need to consult records in order to answer questions about labour turnover, absenteeism and periodical recruitment.

When time is short. At the University of Melbourne in May 1974 it became necessary to obtain information about the child care needs of students and staff. As the matter was urgent there was no time to arrange interviews. Moreover it would not have been possible, without asking more than 10 000 people, to find out who was concerned with this problem. Posters were exhibited on the campus and people with pre-school children were invited to complete questionnaires. The number of respondents reached 92 in six days but it is not possible to say what proportion of students and staff with young children this represented.

Notes

[1]H. Cantril (ed.), *Gauging public opinion,* Princeton University Press, Princeton, N.J., 1944.

[2]Goodchild, *op. cit.*

[3]Cantril, *op. cit.,* p. 45.

[4]Hyman *et al., op. cit.,* p. 133.

[5]M.J. Shapiro, 'Discovering interviewer bias in open-ended survey responses', *Public Opinion Quarterly,* vol. 34, 1970, pp. 412-15.

[6]W.A. Collins, 'Interviewers' verbal idiosyncracies as a source of bias', *Public Opinion Quarterly,* vol. 34, 1970, pp. 416-22.

[7]H. Schuman & J.M. Converse, 'The effects of black and white interviewers on black responses in 1968', *Public Opinion Quarterly,* vol. 35, 1971, pp. 44-68.

[8]Robb, *op. cit.,* p.5.

[9]*ibid.*

[10]From J. Durbin & A. Stuart, 'Callbacks and clustering in sample surveys: an experimental study', *Journal of the Royal Statistical Society,*

Series A, vol. 117, no. 4, 1954, pp. 387-428.

[11]B.S. Dohrenwend, 'An experimental study of directive interviewing', *Public Opinion Quarterly,* vol. 34, 1970, pp. 117-25.

[12]Gans, 1962, *op. cit.*

[13]Dohrenwend, *op. cit.*

[14]M. Schofield, *Sociological aspects of homosexuality: a comparative study of three types of homosexuals,* London, Longmans, 1965; *The sexual behaviour of young people,* Longmans, London (rev. edn Penguin, Harmondsworth, 1968); *Social research,* Heinemann (Concept Books, No. 8), London, 1969; and *The strange case of pot,* Penguin, Harmondsworth, 1971.

[15]E.E. Maccoby & N. Maccoby, ch. 12 'The interview: a tool of social science' in Lindzey, 1954, p. 483.

[16]S.A. Stouffer, L. Guttman, E.A. Suchman, P.F. Lazarsfeld, S.A. Star & J.A. Clausen, *Studies in social psychology in World War II,* vol. IV, *Measurement and prediction,* Princeton University Press, Princeton, N.J., 1950., pp. 719, 721.

[17]C. Scott, 'Research on mail surveys', *Journal of the Royal Statistical Society,* A, vol. 124, 1961, pp. 143-205.

[18]Sources: Opinion polls — the *Australian,* 1 June 1974; actual results — Electoral Office, Canberra, and (final figures) the *Age,* 7 June 1974.

[19]Lord Horder, Letter to the editor 'The General Practitioner and lay education in cancer', *Lancet,* vol. 2, 1953, p. 137.

[20]C.A. Moser, *Survey methods in social investigation,* Heinemann, London, 1958, p. 179.

Further reading

The advantages and disadvantages of using mail (or 'mailed') question-naires and interviews are discussed in Goode & Hatt, 1952; Hyman, 1954; and Moser & Kalton, 1971.

Methodological problems are frequently considered in the *Public Opinion Quarterly.*

Chapter 8
Sampling Methods

'They've never asked me what *I* think.' This is a common complaint and reflects the belief that nothing short of a complete coverage can be valid. In some ways it would be much more satisfying for the researcher to include everyone. There would be no sampling error and therefore no argument about generalising from a part to the whole population. The people themselves would have spoken.

Though it would seem desirable to put our questions to everybody in the survey population, in practice this is seldom possible. Fortunately it has been demonstrated that it is also not necessary. A sample survey, if conducted systematically, can produce results that accurately represent the survey population. Asking everybody can be a waste of time, effort, and money, when using a sample can achieve reliable and accurate results. In fact a sample may give more accurate results than an inefficient attempt to cover everybody. Concentration on a smaller number means that the quality of the data becomes more important than the quantity. Greater accuracy is possible through increased preparation, paying more attention to drafting and pre-testing questions, fuller training of field staff and the inclusion of more thorough checking procedures. Because more time can be spent in contacting specified individuals, the resulting response rate should be higher. If desirable, more time can be spent on each person in order to produce more elaborate information and the elaboration of finer points.

These advantages apply to any form of sampling. In addition, with some sampling methods there are further gains.

If the researcher is aiming to draw conclusions only about the sample itself, any kind of sample will serve the purpose. But if the intention is to draw conclusions about a larger population, of which the sample is only a part, then the sample must be representative of that larger population. Few samples will be perfectly representative but the more representative they are, the greater is the confidence in the conclusions drawn about the larger population.

In essence, to be representative of its population, a sample must be completely random. Not all samples are random and many may only look as if they are. Speaking to the next person you meet is not random; casual interviews in the street are not necessarily random though the interviewer may believe that the people to be interviewed were chosen 'randomly' Despite what the dictionary may tell you, 'random' (in the sense used for sampling) is not the same as 'haphazard'. In sampling terms 'random' means that the selection of units for the sample must be without bias; no person must have a greater chance of being selected than any other person. The person nearest to you does have a better chance than other people and selection of that person, merely because he happens to be nearest, would not be random.

Here it is necessary to pause in order to restate and partially elaborate the main points so far.

1.   Samples can be more economical, less time-consuming, and more accurate than larger numbers such as total populations.

2.   Conclusions can be drawn about any sample without attempting to generalise to a larger population.

3.   If it is hoped to draw conclusions about a larger population, the sample must be representative.

4.   The only way in which we can obtain a sample which is representative *in all respects* is to use some form of random sampling.

This last point needs further explanation and a warning. It is possible by means of a system called **quota sampling** (to be described later) to obtain a sample that is representative in some known respects such as age, sex, and social class. But unless the units are chosen randomly there is a danger of getting a sample that is not representative in other respects, especially as regards unknown factors such as activities, attitudes and opinions. It is possible to check some samples, by comparing them with census figures or other data, to see how representative they are in terms of known population characteristics; there is usually no way of checking for other characteristics when the parameters are unknown.

And now for the warning. Although a random selection provides our only hope of getting a sample that is representative in all respects (point 4 above), a random selection is no guarantee that the sample will be representative even in known respects. It can happen by chance, as with any normal distribution of possibilities, that the sample is way out at one extreme or the other. For instance, if you were to take a sample of 100 students at a university where men outnumber women by two to one, then you would expect to get about thirty three women in the sample. But what if your random sample only contained six women? Obviously it is unbalanced. What should you do? To be on the safe side, consult your friendly statistician and discuss whether you should compensate by using weights (this will restore the balance and can normally save the situation if the discrepancy is not excessive); or draw a fresh sample (after replacement, that is, after putting back into the pool those units previously drawn).

Clearly, social scientists have a preference for random samples, but non-random samples do have a place in the exploratory stages of an investigation; or when wider generalisations are not required; or when the extra time and effort required for random selection is not justified. A newspaper reporter, for instance, may wish to arouse interest rather than claim scientific accuracy.

A random sample enables the researcher to claim that the findings apply to a wider population of the same kind as the sample. Moreover, the margin of error can be estimated and the chances of being wrong (or of the true value being outside this margin) can be stated numerically. This is the notion of confidence levels which will be explained more fully in the chapter on analysis and interpretation of results (Chapter 10).

Principles of random and probability sampling

Random sampling and probability sampling are almost synonymous terms: they share the same basic principles. The first principle is that each unit or element in the population must have an equal chance of being included in the sample. Obviously this chance must be better than zero.

Unless the population is divided into different categories (or strata) such as men and women, all units must, as stated, have an equal chance. But in some circumstances the proportion chosen from one category may differ from the proportion chosen from another — for example, one in ten of all women and one in twenty of all men. Nevertheless the probability must be equal within each category; no man may have a greater chance than any other man of being chosen and likewise for women. In effect, if we do this, men and women are being regarded as belonging to separate populations and the principle of equal chance still holds.

I have deliberately simplified this explanation of the first principle of probability sampling. In effect, this requirement for sampling (that each unit has the same probability of selection) is equivalent to the requirement that all possible samples of the same size must have the same probability of selection. In practice this means that each unit has the same probability of being selected. It is perhaps easier to visualise sampling in terms of the possible fate of the units rather than of the possible samples. Consequently it is easier to accept the essential prerequisite that each unit must be included once and only once in the sampling frame (that is the list, register or pool from which the sample is to be drawn).

The second principle is that the selection must be determined entirely by chance — units must be chosen at random, hence the term 'random sampling'. As already explained, this does not mean that units may be chosen haphazardly, casually or carelessly. There are appropriate procedures, to be described later, that aim to satisfy this second principle and ensure a random selection.

These two principles together lay down the conditions for drawing a random sample. If, *in addition,* the chance or possibility of being included is known, that is, the *probability* can be specified, the procedure qualifies as probability sampling.

Thus a distinction can be made between probability sampling and random sampling according to whether or not we know the size of the population. It would be possible to take a random sample of coffee beans (say, by using the equivalent of a lottery drum) without knowing how many beans were in the sack. This would be a random sample but not a probability sample since without knowing the total size of the population (the number of beans in the sack) the probability cannot be calculated. Sampling supermarket shoppers could be done this way, or taking an approximate 10 per cent sample of marching demonstrators in the United Kingdom[1] or a sample of supporters at a Sydney anti-war rally[2].

It can be argued that probability sampling is a superior form of random sampling. With probability sampling we have more information, namely the size of the population and the sampling ratio, that is, the probability of selection of the units. This means that margins of error can be estimated more accurately by using what is called a **finite population correction**[3]. The effect of neglecting this correction is to overestimate the range of possible error in the results, making us more cautious perhaps than we need be. No great harm in that! For most purposes the difference between random and probability sampling is ignored and the term 'random sampling' is often used loosely to include probability sampling.

To recapitulate:

Probability sampling: The first principle is that each unit in the population has a *known* chance (greater than zero) of being included in the sample; within each population, or each category used as a separate population, each unit has an *equal* chance. Secondly, the selection of units must be random.

From this definition, the notion of **non-probability sampling** follows quite logically.

Non-probability sampling: There is no way of estimating the probability that each unit has of being included in the sample, and consequently no way of estimating margins of error which takes the sampling ratio into account. As shown above, this applies to some forms of random sampling if the size of the population is unknown. Moreover this applies to all forms of non-random sampling because, in those cases, the probability of selection of each unit is unknowable, even if the population size is known. For some units like the beans at the top of the undisturbed sack, it will be very high, and for the rest it will be much lower; how high or how low cannot be estimated.

Rather more serious perhaps is the fact that in non-random sampling there is no assurance that every unit has *some* chance of being included; and some units, which might vary in important respects from others, might have an unfair chance of turning up in the sample. The result of these uncertainties regarding exclusion and inclusion is that we can have very little confidence that the sample will be representative.

So with *non-probability sampling* the exact probability of selection is unknown. With **non-random sampling** there is no assurance that every unit has a chance of being included; some units may even have more chance than they should have; either way the sample would be biased and not representative.

In order to appreciate the merits of random sampling let us look at some non-random methods before going through the various forms of probability sampling.

Non-random sampling methods

As already explained, these may also be regarded as forms of non-probability sampling.

Accidental samples

These are made up of people who happen to be available, or volunteer, or are easily reached because their names are in the telephone book or some other restricted directory.

The classic example of a straw vote that did not detect the direction of the wind was the attempt to forecast the USA Presidential election in 1936. The *Literary Digest* sent out 10 million questionnaires and received 2 376 000 replies showing that Roosevelt would get 43 per cent of the votes. In fact he obtained 61 per cent. The error was due to bad sampling: names were selected from car registration and telephone directories. The response rate was less than 25 per cent; only willing volunteers bothered to reply and they were self-selected and not random; they were not even representative of the middle and upper classes. Sample size is not everything. As we said previously, when discussing the disadvantages of questionnaires, volunteers are self-selected and often not typical or representative; they tend to be better educated, have higher social status, be more interested in the survey topic, and to have more leisure.

Quota samples (a form of judgment sampling)

This is one of the most severely criticised forms of sampling, yet it is widely used and has many advocates. The aim of quota sampling is certainly attractive since it makes a deliberate attempt to include a cross-section of the community under study — that is, one that 'represents' the population. Hence quota samples are sometimes mistakenly called 'representative' samples. Under ideal conditions they would be truly representative but in practice too much depends upon the 'judgment' of the interviewer.

The procedure begins with the known characteristics of the population as shown by census or other figures. The population is tabulated in terms of social class, sex, and age groups (or whatever **control variables** are considered important for the survey). In order to ensure that the sample will have the correct proportions, not only of men and women but of rich and poor, young women and older women, and so on, quotas are drawn up that specify how many of each category the sample should contain. This constitutes the Master Quota Sheet. Each category may be broken down into sub-categories, for example according to age. These figures might be the nearest whole number to 1 per cent of the total in each of the sub-categories. The figures in the Master Quota are then divided, sometimes approximately, by the number of interviewers, so that the resulting quota sheet might look like this.

EXAMPLE OF INTERVIEWER'S QUOTA SHEET

Social Class	Men		Women		Total
	Aged 21-39	Aged 40 & over	Aged 21-39	Aged 40 & over	
Upper & U-Middle	2	1	1	1	5
Middle	4	4	5	6	19
Lower	3	3	3	3	12
Total	9	8	9	10	36

The proportions for each sub-category or cell need not be the same for all cells. For example, in the first column '2' might be the nearest whole number to 5 per cent of all the upper- and middle-class men aged 21-39, whereas '4' might be close to 1 per cent, and '3' close to 2 per cent of the middle- and lower-class men of that age in what would be a predominantly middle-class area. If you want to generalise from your sample to the whole population, you may have to adjust the results so that the correct proportions of the various sub-groups are maintained. This is done by applying appropriate weights. In this example, dividing the total survey results in the first cell by five and in the third cell by two would produce the equivalent of a 1 per cent sample. A uniform representation could also be obtained by multiplication: results in the three cells would be multiplied by 1, 5, and 2½. These figures are only approximate because the cell numbers were obtained by taking the nearest whole number; the exact weights, whether dividing or multiplying, would depend on the precise percentage of the sample in the sub-category compared with the total population in that sub-category. Another method of weighting is to multiply the results in each cell by the inverse of the sampling ratio; for example 5 per cent is one in twenty or 1/20 and the three cells would be multiplied by 20, 100, and 50 respectively.

However, if there are large differences between categories in the way they answer some items, it is better to give the separate figures rather than an overall figure that can be misleading. For instance, if 60 per cent of the women and 30 per cent of the men oppose a city redevelopment proposal, it is essential to report this. To give a weighted average (which might be close to 45 per cent) and say that the majority of people are not opposed to the scheme could conceal an important division of opinion even though the average might be numerically correct.

When comparisons are made within the sample, say between category 'A' (men) and category 'B' (women), the survey results can be used without correction even though 5 per cent of the women and a different proportion of the men (say 1 per cent) were interviewed. But in that case the results for the women must be based on a sample that has the same sampling proportion for all the sub-categories of women and likewise for the men.

If the interviewer selects respondents conscientiously and successfully, quota sampling ensures an adequate representation of all sections; but the more specific the instructions become, the more difficult it is for the interviewers to find their subjects. This puts too much strain upon the honesty of the interviewer.

Too much is left to the discretion of the interviewer — kinds of people he likes or dislikes, parts of town; he may find the hotel bar a good place for interviewing men; people who are out may be missed — and much depends upon his assessment of age, income group and so on.

In the example of a quota sheet given above, the required subjects are classified in three ways — social class, sex, and age: that is to say the controls are *interrelated*. To make the job easier for the interviewer, an alternative scheme using *independent* controls could be used. The quota sheet would then look like this.

Sex		Age		Class	
Male	17	21-39	18	Upper	5
Female	19	40+	18	Middle	19
	36			Lower	12

The total in each category is still the same as in the first example; there are 17 men and 19 women of whom 18 are in each age group and the social class totals are as before, but the sub-categories (e.g. number of middle-class men aged 21-39) are left undefined. Therefore, until a category such as sex, age, or social class is completed, the interviewer has more freedom in choosing subjects. Unfortunately, pairing the controls can produce some imbalance. For example, the interviewer could interview 17 middle-class males aged 21-39 — a gross distortion compared with the 4 such respondents specified by the proportional quota sample given on p. 93. Such extreme imbalance would defeat the aim of obtaining a truly representative sample.

For quota sampling to work at all, two things are necessary: reliable statistics and reliable interviewers.

Reliable statistics on the control variables of the specific survey population (and not just the larger population in general) are a prime necessity. These may be available if only the independent control type of quota is required and if the survey population can be delineated to correspond to census collectors' districts. But there could be some difficulty in obtaining the appropriate sub-category proportions for interrelated control quotas.

Reliable interviewers must be found who can make sound and honest judgments about complete strangers. The sex and age categories are easiest to handle but social class is becoming increasingly less discernible. If the first guess is not confirmed, an interviewer must be honest enough to pass on to another subject if necessary and not bend the personal data to fit cell vacancies. Even if the interviewer is diligent and persists in searching for appropriate individuals, the availability of people to be interviewed will still remain a dominant factor in selection.

The availability factor prevails even with more sophisticated methods of quota sampling that attempt to inject some control over the interviewer. The method described by Sudman[4] as 'probability sampling with quotas' uses tight geographical controls that must be followed by each interviewer. In filling a quota the interviewer follows specified travel patterns, calling at pre-designated households (say every third house) as in area sampling (p. 102) until the quota is filled. This considerably restricts the interviewer's latitude of choice, but the major advantage claimed for this procedure may be speed.

If the interviewer has too much latitude of choice, there is a double non-random selection effect. The interviewer is relatively free to select a 'suitable' respondent who may agree (and so 'volunteer') or not agree to be interviewed. The interviewer continues in this way until the quota is completed. I have found that if university students are free to choose which door they knock, they tend to pick subjects nearer their own type, even within the quota social sub-groups. Their samples tend to be inadequate at the top end of the upper-class bracket and at the lower end of the unskilled group. Mann[5] found that when his 239 students were each given a quota of six respondents to interview within the suburb of their own residence there were similar sample bias effects. Interrelated controls of sex and three age groups (18-30, 31-45, 46 and over) were used and own family, friends, or acquaintances were excluded; only one respondent could be drawn from any one family. Comparison with census statistics showed that the resulting sample overrepresented the 20-24 year olds and underrepresented all ages above 50 years. People with university and other tertiary education were highly overrepresented, people with secondary education were slightly overrepresented, while people with primary education were underrepresented.

Purposive samples (another form of judgment sampling)

A sample can be made up of people or units specially selected for a particular purpose; those selected are supposed to be typical. But how do we know that they really are typical, and in all respects?

The town or suburb is selected because it is judged to be typical of a certain kind of community. In one of my unpublished surveys six areas were chosen — two each (old and new) working-class, middle-class, and upper-class areas. The Lancaster Jones Index of social stratification[6] was used and a town-planning consultant gave advice on suitable old and new pairs within the three social class groupings. Thus the six survey populations were chosen on a comparative basis.

Probability sampling methods

As already stated, the basic principle is that every element in the survey population has a known chance, greater than zero, of being included in the sample; secondly, the selection is determined entirely by chance. The following methods are regarded as probability sampling on the assumption that the chance of selection is known, that is, the probability of any unit being chosen can be specified.

Simple random samples

Each element has an equal chance of being selected. Moreover every possible combination of the desired number of cases is equally likely.

The process of selection is similar to the lottery method, but instead of drawing names from a hat or numbered discs from an urn, random numbers are used. For example, if we require a sample of 400 from a population of 12 000 we would take a numbered list (each person included only once) and from a table of random numbers draw 400 different numbers, beginning of course from some random starting point.

Drawing *different* numbers precludes the possibility of some people appearing in the sample more than once. This seems sensible but most statistical theory is built on a procedure known as 'sampling with replacement'. This produces unrestricted random samples in which a person or unit can appear more than once.

The difference between sampling without replacement (simple random samples) and sampling with replacement (unrestricted random samples) need cause no concern here. These methods are seldom used in practice but the general principles behind them form the basis for the various modifications resulting in more complicated designs.

Systematic random samples

If the survey population is very large, numbering every unit and selecting a sample by using random numbers can be very laborious. Fortunately it is unnecessary. A systematic random sample can be obtained from a list simply by counting, without numbering the items first. Because units are selected from a list or file, the method is sometimes called **file sampling.**

This method requires a complete up-to-date list or register that includes everyone who is entitled to be included: there must be one and only one entry per person. If a sample of 400 is required from a population of 12 000, then every thirtieth name is taken. The interval depends on the sampling ratio. The starting point is decided by chance — in this case by taking a number between 1 and 30 (both inclusive) from a table of random numbers.

The best type of list would be one in which the entries are random. Probably an alphabetical list, though not perfect, comes close to being random. One could of course shuffle or scramble the list to be on the safe side. Otherwise there may be a trend or bias, which for some surveys could be serious.

Employees in a factory, for example, may be registered sequentially upon being engaged to work: their time-card or clock numbers could also reflect this rank order of seniority. A sample beginning 1, 31, 61 . . . 2971 would differ from another sample 30, 60, 90 . . . 3000 (to take the extreme case in this example). In the first sample each unit chosen would have more seniority than his counterpart in the second sample by 29 ranks.

Instead of showing a trend, the list may have a cyclical fluctuation. For example, the list may be grouped in tens (perhaps work sections) and each group of ten may be listed in order of seniority; there are thirty possible samples — three of these samples (those with the random starts of 1, 11, or 21) would select the most senior employee in each group of 10; three others the most junior; and the other samples would fluctuate similarly.

In a community that was built according to a systematic plan, the list of houses in order of streets and numbers would contain corner houses at regular intervals. Therefore some samples might contain only corner houses and other samples would contain no corner houses. In either case the results would be misleading if the corner houses were larger and more expensive than the others. It is likely also that their occupants would differ in certain characteristics.

Though systematic random samples are more vulnerable than simple random samples to cyclic or periodic listing and trends, they do ensure a more even spread of units. They are used quite extensively, especially for homogeneous populations. Where heterogeneity has to be taken into account and may even be a centre of special interest, a stratified sample would be more appropriate.

Stratified random samples

This method involves the prior division or classification of the survey population into sub-populations called **strata.** Every sampling unit must be placed in one (and only one) of the strata before selecting the sample. Stratification can be done on the basis of categories such as age, sex, income, social class, occupation, or whatever is considered relevant to the subject matter of the survey. In this respect it is rather like quota sampling and both methods aim to include proper proportions of the various sections in the community. But here the similarity ends, because for stratified random samples the selection is made within each stratum separately using a random procedure. Therefore, within strata, each unit has a known chance of being selected. In contrast, according to Moser and Kalton[7] quota sampling is 'a method of stratified sampling in which the selection within strata is non-random'. This is because selection depends on the judgment of the interviewer and also upon convenience and accident — who happens to be around when the interviewer is looking for respondents. Because it is non-random, quota sampling cannot specify the probability of selection. Thus it can be claimed that stratified random samples are superior. They qualify as probability sampling not only because the units within each stratum are randomly selected in a proper manner, but also because the probability of any unit being chosen is known.

In stratified random sampling two decisions must first be made: how to select the important and relevant divisions; and whether to use equal or unequal proportions.

The first decision depends on the nature of the problem. If it is thought that young people have different opinions about sports facilities than older people, then age would be an obvious factor for stratification. But in other cases the strata may not be so obvious. Take, for example, the proposal to construct a giant regional shopping complex at Hornsby in the centre of Sydney's crowded northern access corridor.[8] How would the survey populations be defined for the purpose of a project impact study?

How would the relevant divisions or strata be determined? Distance could be one factor; opinions of those living in immediate proximity to the site might differ from those living further away, and similarly for those working and those trading. Without the guidance of previous studies (or a sound understanding of local social dynamics) it would be difficult to identify the important factors.

For reasons related to sampling theory, the use of an irrelevant factor as the basis for stratification is a waste of effort. An equal degree of precision would be obtained from a simple random sample.

Even if the relevant factors are known or can be presumed, there is still the problem of knowing how many people belong to each category. Before, say, a one in ten sample can be drawn, or any sampling fraction, we need to know the size of each sub-population. In the Hornsby example these would be

Units	Distance	
households	(a) within a certain radius	(b) further away
workers etc.	ditto	ditto
traders	ditto	ditto

The second decision, to use equal or unequal proportions is not really affected by the desire to achieve representative sampling. For some people 'representative' implies that different parts of the population must be properly represented by using a uniform sampling fraction or ratio (i.e. **proportionate stratified random sample**). To obtain an average for the whole sample, it is not necessary to apply any special weighting procedure — the method is 'self-weighting'.

However, a representative sample can just as well be achieved through disproportionate stratification using a variable sampling ratio. In some cases a larger sampling ratio might even ensure a more adequate representation of small sub-groups. To obtain an average for the whole sample is quite simple: the results for each stratum are multiplied by the inverse of the sampling ratio. (as explained on page 94 for quota samples.)

Which is the best sampling method?

The relative merits of the two forms of stratification, and of other methods are somewhat technical and it is best to seek the advice of a statistician who specialises in sampling. However a few guidelines are given below.

Situations in which you would use a variable sampling ratio **(disproportionate stratification)** —

(a) Strictly proportional sampling may produce a very small number of cases for a given stratum; or in extreme cases fractions of units or even less than one.

(b) When an important stratum contains a smaller number of units, a higher sampling ratio would be advisable. In a survey of shopping facilities it may be necessary to include all the large stores and a sample of the remainder.

(c) The form of stratification (equal or variable sampling ratios) is not so important if only overall estimates of the population are required. But usually more than this is possible and desirable. The special sub-groups are often of interest in themselves and for comparisons with other sub-groups. Therefore it is important to have an adequate sample from each sub-group.

If a stratum is likely to be subdivided for further analysis, a higher proportion of cases from this stratum should be obtained in the sample. The use of a fixed sampling ratio might provide insufficient cases in this stratum to permit subdivision.

(d) Variability of characteristics or expected responses within a stratum will affect the choice of stratification method. The greater the homogeneity within a stratum, the smaller is the sample required for a given degree of precision. Therefore if considerable variation is expected within a certain stratum, then a larger sample will be required from that stratum to produce the same degree of precision. The greater the variability in the stratum, the higher must be the sampling ratio if an acceptable level of accuracy is to be reached. The use of a variable sampling ratio can take into account differences in stratum homogeneity.

(e) If data collection costs are an important consideration then it might be worth using smaller sampling ratios in those strata where costs are unduly high.

But how would you be able to decide about using a variable sampling ratio *before* taking a sample?

Many of the points relating to decisions about sampling depend on having some prior information. The relevant factors for stratification may not be known with any certainty. Available census figures or official records may not have been analysed in accordance with these factors and some idea of the total number of units in each category would be needed. The choice of suitable sampling ratios depends on knowing these category sizes and may also depend on knowing what variability to expect within each category or stratum. If the differences between classes (or strata) are greater than the differences *within* classes (the classes themselves being internally relatively homogeneous) then some form of stratification is advisable.

Probable sources of information or guidance would include previous surveys covering similar topics or similar populations. If these are not available and helpful experts are not accessible, then it may be that conducting a pilot study or a series of pilot studies would be the only solution. And that's not a bad solution anyway. One of the most important functions of the pilot survey is to provide information that will improve both the questioning and the sampling procedures.

Combining these methods

So far three methods of probability sampling have been described. The basic procedure was **simple random sampling** with selection by random numbers; the more usual method of **systematic random sampling** selects units at intervals, beginning at a random point; thirdly, **stratified random sampling** was described, in which the survey population can be regarded as a number of sub-populations and a decision made to use either a constant or a variable sampling ratio. The possible combinations of these methods are shown below. This shows that if the survey population is treated as a whole (unstratified) the sampling ratio must be constant but the method of random selection may be either simple or systematic. If the survey population is stratified then the sampling ratio may be constant or variable and in each case the method of random selection may again be either simple or systematic.

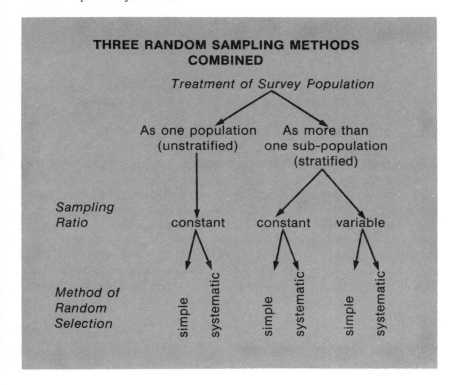

Selection of units is usually made from a list or register but there are often cases in which no suitable list exists or the lists do not contain sufficient details for stratification. The electoral register, for example, may indicate sex (first names) and social class (residential address) but gives no information about age, occupation, or ethnic grouping. Other sampling methods and refinements are intended to meet these difficulties and will be considered now.

Area sampling — random samples from maps

Area sampling is an important kind of listing procedure which is widely used in social surveys. People are chosen according to place rather than file or list, for example, every *N*th residence beginning at a randomly chosen spot. Unlike file sampling an exact up-to-date register of residents is not required because a direct sample of current residents is obtained. Nothing is left to the choice or judgment of the interviewers: providing they are persistent (if people are out or reluctant to participate) and do not substitute houses or respondents, and providing instructions are specific and carried out honestly, then a truly random sample of actual residents should be obtained.

These instructions should define carefully and exactly

> (a) What is a 'residence' or 'shop' or whatever the basis of the sample is;
> (b) Who should be interviewed — not necessarily the first person who comes to the door as this would result in a biased sample;
> (c) The route to be taken — in what direction from the first point and whether to go round corners or to complete one street first;
> (d) What to do if a person is out — how many times and when to call back.

This last point can make area sampling very time-consuming and therefore very expensive. After calling back the required number of times without success, the interviewer may be permitted to substitute — again, according to instructions.

Substitutes in this, as in any form of sampling, must be obtained by using the same procedure that is adopted for the whole sample.

Area sampling is very useful in rapidly growing areas or where residential turnover is high and where electoral registers quickly become out of date. If the street maps themselves are not sufficiently recent the survey team may have to do some preliminary mapping or commission an aerial survey.

Cluster and multi-stage sampling

To cover a large area, such as a town, area sampling would involve walking large distances between house calls, especially with a sampling ratio of, say, 1 in 100. The use of cars would increase field costs considerably. To meet this difficulty the survey area may be divided into sub-areas or blocks (for example by drawing a grid on the map) and a number of blocks can then be selected at random. This method is known as 'clustering' or **cluster sampling:** the clusters may be regarded as the sampling units.

However it may not be necessary to include in the sample every household in each cluster chosen. After randomly selecting the clusters, area sampling can be used for sampling within these clusters. This is known as **multi-stage sampling**. Providing the clusters are reasonably comparable in size (i.e. contain about the same number of sampling units), a sampling ratio of 1 in 100 can be achieved by first selecting 1 in 10 of the clusters and then calling on 1 in 10 of the units in these clusters.

Multi-stage sampling may involve two or more stages and is not confined to area sampling (nor to probability sampling generally). But area sampling is most readily combined with this method because of the ease with which maps can be subdivided by grids or by the use of natural boundaries.

Lowering field costs has already been mentioned as a good reason for clustering. A further reason would be to overcome the absence of a proper list for the whole population which is needed as a sampling frame. The clusters, blocks, or areas could be chosen before listing all the relevant units, and then the work of listing would only be necessary for the selected clusters.

Stratified cluster sampling

Stratification would be necessary if the survey area varied considerably from one part to another. For instance there could be old and new areas, considerable social class differences, and industrial, residential, and shopping districts. If the land use formed a patterned rather than a random distribution or was zoned for planning purposes, then an adequate representation of each type of area would be desirable in a survey covering the city or country. This could be obtained either by stratified cluster sampling or by using a fine grid (and thus small blocks) for a systematic sample.

Multi-phase sampling

It is sometimes necessary to locate a population within a population. The whole sample is asked for basic data together with one or a few items which will identify those who belong to the group in which we are particularly interested. These may be: elderly people; families with pre-school children; people wanting to move; people who travel a long way to work; and so on.

Depending on how many people there are in our special category and depending on our resources, we may decide to interview all of them or a sample of them (or send them a second questionnaire). This is **multi-phase**

sampling — whether we approach all of them or not. In other words, we ask some people (those belonging to our special category) for more information; in the second phase, the sub-sample is asked a set of special questions.

The difference between this and multi-stage sampling should be clear though the two methods can be used in conjunction. With multi-stage sampling we move from broad sampling units (whole towns perhaps) to houses or people; whereas in multi-phase sampling the type of sampling unit remains constant but the intensity of questioning increases.

Of course the full questionnaire could be sent out in the first place, with a suitable filter item. This could be expensive and the people who are not the special subject of our interest may feel it unnecessary to reply since most of the questions are not relevant to them. Then again we may want to interview the sub-sample (second phase) and so a very short questionnaire will suffice for the first phase and will encourage a higher response rate.

Two other purposes of multi-phase sampling may be mentioned briefly. The first phase can be used to obtain a general picture of the population as a basis for stratification. For example the frequency and location of people with different levels of education, or type and size of residence can be tabulated. Secondly, if the second phase does not produce a 100 per cent response, through our failure to contact them or their lack of co-operation, we at least have the basic information. The sources and possible effects of non-response can thus be estimated to some extent.

In the Melbourne Poverty Survey 4000 people were interviewed for ten to twenty minutes in the first phase; of these, 500 were selected for a second interview of two hours. This second phase consisted mostly of people described on the basis of the first interview as living in or near poverty. A few families with higher incomes were re-interviewed for comparative purposes.[9]

Clustering and the cost of the survey

As was previously mentioned, clustering results in the more economical use of resources in the work of going from house to house in order to obtain interviews and in this way can lower the costs of the survey. As might be expected, some types of clustering may be more economical than others. This problem was investigated experimentally by Durbin and Stuart who found that 'clustering by polling districts had the effect of reducing interviewing costs by about one-third'. Contrary to expectation, the further reduction of the size of the clusters by taking streets as the units was more expensive than clustering by polling districts. 'Both types of clustering, however, gave lower costs per interview than systematic scattering over the entire towns'.[10] Of course costs are not everything, so they also looked to see whether there was any loss of accuracy due to the type of clustering used. Taking into account both accuracy and costs, they found that clustering by districts was more efficient than clustering by streets[11]. The survey they carried out for this experiment was not concerned with local issues so their findings would not necessarily apply to all social surveys. Most of the questions they used (for example, those relating to smoking, watching television, reading) were not affected by the streets in which the respondents lived. But those items that related to types of newspapers which were read, film-going, owning a car, gardening, age of house and age of respondent, all indicated that people living relatively close together gave similar answers that contrasted with answers obtained in different streets or localities. In choosing the units for clustering, any possible effect of locality would have to be considered. Durbin and Stuart point out that they selected their polling districts at random and that stratification of the polling districts might have improved the efficiency of clustering.[12]

These are the main methods of sampling suitable for social surveys. Many different combinations are possible, some of which have been mentioned. But there are still some more general problems involved in sampling. These will be dealt with in the next chapter.

Notes

[1]F. Parkin, *Middle class radicalism: the social bases of the British campaign for nuclear disarmament,* Melbourne University Press, 1968.

[2]L. Mann, 'Attitudes towards My Lai and obedience to orders: an Australian survey', *Australian Journal of Psychology,* vol. 25, no. 1, April 1973, pp. 11-21.

[3]W.G. Cochran, *Sampling techniques,* Wiley, New York, 2nd edn, 1966, p. 17; M.H. Hansen, W.N. Hurwitz & W.G. Madow, *Sample survey methods and theory, Vol. I: Methods and applications,* Wiley, New York, 1953, pp. 122-26.

[4]S. Sudman, *Reducing the cost of surveys,* Aldine Publishing Co., Chicago, 1967.

[5]Mann, *op. cit.*

[6]Jones, 1967, *op. cit.;* and by the same author *Dimensions of urban social structure,* ANU Press, Canberra, 1969.

[7]Moser & Kalton, *op. cit.,* p. 127.

[8]*National Times,* 5-10 August 1974, pp. 28, 29.

[9]R.F. Henderson, A. Harcourt & R.J.A. Harper, *People in poverty: a Melbourne survey,* Cheshire, for the Institute of Applied Economic and Social Research, University of Melbourne, 1970.

[10]Durbin & Stuart, *op. cit.,* p. 402.

[11]*ibid.,* p. 406.

[12]*ibid.,* p. 407.

Further reading

The statistical aspects of sampling are best left to the expert. Kish believes that they should come as the third course of study after one on the fundamentals of statistical reasoning and another on major statistical tools (Kish, 1965, preface). A similar progression seems advisable in further reading about sampling methods. The following three classifications are arranged in order of length and difficulty (which appear to be positively correlated) but I make no distinction within each category.

Introductory chapters: Bartholomew & Bassett, 1971, ch. 11; I. Chein's chapter (pp. 546-74) in Selltiz *et. al.,* 1960; Goode & Hatt, 1952, ch. 14; L. Kish (ch. 5) in Festinger & Katz, 1953.

Intermediate chapters: B. Lazerwitz (ch. 8) in Blalock & Blalock, 1968; Moser & Kalton, 1971, chs 4, 5, 6.

Advanced books: Hansen *et al.,* 1953, vol. I; Kish, 1965; Yates, 1960.

Chapter 9

Some General Problems in Sampling

Choosing the appropriate sampling methods does not solve everything. The full implementation of the survey design will depend upon how successfully a number of problems are overcome. These problems are liable to cause trouble whatever sampling method is intended.

Defining the sampling unit

Sampling involves selecting part of a population, to represent the whole population. Therefore the sampling units must be defined in the same way as the population, otherwise we cannot generalise about the whole population on the basis of our sample. There are other restrictions to making generalisations but this one is basic. One cannot make valid generalisations about a population composed of different races or ethnic origins, or of different cultural backgrounds, if the sampling units exclude any one of these different groups. This exclusion could be an effect of the way in which the sampling units are defined or the method of selection.

Sampling units, whether individuals, households, or areas, must be clearly and unambiguously defined. The definition will determine the actual survey population which may or may not correspond exactly to the population that was originally intended.

In the series of surveys covering students at the University of Melbourne[1] the samples had to be delimited in a number of ways. The study began with the aim of finding out to what extent university students were interested in politics, demonstrations, student activities, and issues such as student involvement in university matters. It was decided to concentrate on a fairly homogeneous population in terms of the possible amount of daily contact with other students at the university and opportunities to participate in campus activities. Stratification on this basis might have been fruitful but would have been difficult and possibly cumbersome. Therefore we excluded part-time students and those enrolled for higher degrees and diplomas. Students with the Royal

Australian Air Force Academy spend most of their time away from the Melbourne campus and were excluded for this reason. Finally students from overseas often feel under some constraint about becoming involved in Australian politics and it was thought inadvisable to include them in the sample.

The subjects of the survey (sampling units) were defined as *Students at the University of Melbourne, normally resident in Australia, enrolled and currently pursuing a full-time undergraduate course of study other than through the RAAF Academy*. This also defines the survey population. Notice how the process of definition begins with a general concept or universe of interest ('university students') which is modified according to what is feasible and advisable — what sampling units can in fact be obtained — until it is possible to redefine the population in accordance with these sampling units.

This is a form of operational definition. In social science it is often necessary to define a concept (such as 'intelligence' or 'leadership') or a category (such as 'working class') by reference to the operations that are used to measure it. The danger of this procedure is the possibility of going into reverse without even noticing what is happening. Operationism in reverse would be to talk or write as though, for instance, all that we ever mean by 'intelligence' is the score obtained on the test which was chosen to measure intelligence.

The moral is that though our sampling units are defined in a way that suits our purpose we must remember that this is not the only meaning possible. In the Melbourne University surveys just mentioned it would be reasonable to assume, with caution, that the results applied to all university students; but a strict statistical generalisation would be limited to university students as defined in the survey.

The problem of definition may not always be quite as complicated as this example but an important principle is always involved. If a survey of residents of a city or patients in a hospital excludes those who cannot speak English, then the survey population must be defined accordingly.

Sampling frames

One factor that will often enter into the final definition of sampling units will be the availability of suitable sampling frames. These are lists, registers, or other records from which samples are drawn.

If a probability sample is required, then the sampling frame must satisfy the basic requirement that each unit must have a chance of being included in the sample but must not have an unfair chance. This means that each unit must be included once and only once. There must be no omissions and no duplicate entries in the ideal sampling frame.

It is probably true to say that most sampling frames will be defective.

Arrangements will have to be made to meet these deficiencies, either by correcting errors, relisting, or combining lists; finally, in addition it may be necessary to redefine the survey population.

In general it is likely that proposed sampling frames will contain four types of errors: wrong information; too little information; too much information; and inconvenient information.

Wrong information: errors, and out-of-date lists

Some inaccuracies are due to incorrect entries when the lists are made; others arise later when the lists become out of date. This can happen very quickly. By the time the United Kingdom Register of Electors appears it is already four months out of date.

Wrong entries include wrong names and addresses, and non-existing units (for example, people who have moved or died). These errors can usually be discovered and corrected after the sample has been drawn: this would require less work than correcting the whole list before drawing the sample.

Not enough information: incomplete or inadequate

Units may be missing — new residents and new houses may not have been entered. It is difficult to know when a sampling frame is incomplete.

Sometimes lists may serve the purpose for which they were made but be inadequate as a sampling frame. Some categories of units may not be included: for instance people under the age for voting. There are two solutions. One is to combine lists to cover the survey population (taking care to avoid duplication) and the other is to redefine the survey population to correspond to the available sampling frame.

Too much information: duplication, and other unwanted entries

Duplication of entries violates the principle that sampling units shall not have an unfair chance of selection. It is possible for a person's name to appear more than once in a telephone directory. When lists are combined, as suggested above, in order to ensure a complete coverage, there is the chance that duplication will occur. Fortunately this is easy to detect but massive documents like directories might present more of a difficulty.

The introduction of computerised records has simplified the job of eliminating unwanted information. To draw a sample of university students, as defined in the previous section, student enrolment records were used. These included all students — one entry per student. The computer was programmed to disregard all those entries relating to students who came outside the definition and to draw a systematic sample. The restrictions imposed in this way resulted in a sampling frame that exactly corresponded to the defined survey population.

If the sampling frame covers a wider population than the one required it is said to include **foreign elements or blanks.** The sample is drawn in the usual manner but all blanks falling into the sample are just ignored. This means, of course, that the sample will be short of the intended number. To overcome this deficiency it is tempting to take the next eligible unit listed after each blank that is drawn. But this would give those units an unfair second chance of being drawn in the sample after the first run through the list had excluded them. The solution is to relate the sampling ratio to the size or proportion of the eligible units.

An example will make this clear. A 10 per cent sample of women is required from a list of 3365 people. If women comprise about a third of the list, or about 1122, then by taking every tenth name on the list (beginning at a random point of course) we would have about

$$
\begin{array}{rl}
224 & \text{men} \\
\underline{112} & \text{women} \\
336 &
\end{array}
$$

The men are simply ignored as blanks (an unusual fate but appropriate here) leaving 10 per cent of the women as required. Ignoring the unwanted 224 would entail less clerical work than listing the 1122 women separately.

If the proportion of blanks is not known, it can be estimated from a few random sections of the list.

Inconvenient information:

The sampling frame may have all the necessary information, but in an inconvenient form. If the list has a trend or a cycle, a systematic sample would be biased in some way as was shown previously (p. 97).

Another problem would arise if the units are in clusters or groups, just as people are listed according to their addresses. A selection of one person from each address would give some people (those in small households) a greater chance of being selected than people living in large households. The solution depends on whether you are sampling people or households or houses. If in fact the cluster is the sampling unit then it is only a question of deciding which person shall speak for the cluster drawn in the sample. A procedure for doing this will be described later. Drawing a sample of people from clustered listings is quite simple. Sample the clusters (for example, houses) and list all the occupants. Draw a sample from this list.

Other methods, such as interviewing all the occupants of each cluster in the sample, or randomly taking one in each cluster are less satisfactory.

To interview everybody in the house could be tedious and possibly embarrassing for the interviewer. The replies may be unduly similar as the result of respondents actually conferring during the process or because they relate to shared attitudes. In either case the results would be biased. If only one person is chosen as a respondent, the method of analysis would have to take the size of each cluster into account and adjust by weighting.

The size of the sample

Obviously, other things being equal, the accuracy of results depends on the size of the sample — the larger the sample, the better. If the whole population is included then sampling error is eliminated. But experience from forecasting presidential election votes in the USA shows that a 100 per cent sample is not essential providing the sampling is scientific. With sampling ratios as low as 11 out of every 100 000 voters (= 0.011 per cent), accuracy around the 1 per cent error mark has been obtained with district samples of about 5000 electors[2]. The Australian election forecasts (see p. 82) were based on samples of between 0.02 and 0.03 per cent, or 2000 to 2600 electors.

Experience and statistical theory also show that a point of diminishing returns is reached fairly quickly. So there is no sense in wasting money on a larger sample for the sake of a marginal increase in accuracy.

For these reasons one of the questions most frequently asked by newcomers to survey research and which needs to be tackled in any social survey is: 'How large a sample do I need?'

We might just as well ask: 'How long is a piece of string?' or 'How thick is a rope?' It depends what you want to do with it, in each case. The same is true of a sample. How much strain must the sample bear?

There is no magic in any particular percentage though people often seem to think that 5 per cent is somehow respectable. Nor is there a universally ideal size such as 500. However samples of less than 30 or 40, from relatively large populations such as those covered in social surveys, are usually not adequate for statistical analysis. So how do we decide what would be the appropriate size?

The adequacy of the sample will depend mainly upon the degree of accuracy or precision that is required or, in other words, what margin of error we are prepared to accept. Accuracy is estimated by the sampling error or **standard error** of a sample statistic such as an average (mean) or a proportion. For example if 66 in a sample of 100 say they would prefer to shop in the proposed supermarket, and the rest are against or undecided, the standard error would be 4.74. This means that the true level of support in the actual population would probably be in the range 66 ±4.74, that is 61.26 per cent to 70.74 per cent. This range might be too large for practical planning purposes and a larger sample would be required in order to obtain a result with a smaller margin of error, that is, a lower standard error — see opposite.

The standard error will depend on the sample size and it will also depend on the variability of the units under investigation. But here we are in a difficulty. How do we know in advance anything about the variability in the population? In some cases the results of previous surveys may help; a pilot survey would be more up-to-date. One of the purposes of a pilot survey is to give some guidance on sample size for the final survey. Suppose in a pilot survey of fifty citizens, two are against a planning proposal, two are uncertain, and 46 are in favour. We could assume that opinion is overwhelmingly in favour of the planning proposal and only a small final sample of the population would be needed to confirm this. If more precise information is required, such as the exact percentage in favour (within a margin of say 2 per cent either way), then a larger sample would be needed. Now suppose that the pilot survey produced a different result — 16 against, 10 uncertain, and 24 in favour. Clearly a larger final sample would be needed in order to confirm any acceptance of the proposal. Again, how large would depend on the degree of accuracy and level of confidence required. In other words, how much risk of being wrong you are prepared to accept. Only a statistician can tell you how much larger the sample should be in order to meet your requirements.

The table on p. 114 provides a rough guide of the sample size needed depending on opinion variability. The standard error will be lowest when the variability is low, as for the overwhelming majority case shown in column (1); high variability, as in the marginal majority case, will produce nearly twice as much error, as shown in column (2).

It is rather unusual to restrict a survey to a single issue; nearly always there are a number of different issues each involving many questions. The best plan is to set the standard of accuracy required for the most important question or issue in the survey and estimate the sample size on the expected variability for that item. If all items are equally important then the item with the greatest expected variability can be taken as the basis for estimating the sample size which will produce the required level of accuracy.

In the example just given, we can assume that the issue in question was whether the public in general would support or oppose a stated proposal. But it may be necessary to break down the data into a number of different categories. A comparison of men and women would only require two categories; dividing these into three age groups would produce six; and if we now add three occupational groups we end up with eighteen categories. Obviously, the larger the number of categories required for the data analysis, the larger is the sample required.

So far no mention has been made of the non-response rate. Clearly if this is likely to be high, a larger sample will be required.

SAMPLE SIZE AND STANDARD ERROR

Let us suppose that on the basis of a pilot study we expect that about 66 per cent are in favour of a proposed local development. The remainder are either against or undecided; for this illustration they are grouped together.

What will be the probable accuracy or precision of an estimate of the proportion in favour based on samples of different sizes? The standard error provides an estimate of this precision.

Assuming each time that 66 per cent are in favour, the standard errors would be as follows:

Sample size (n)	Standard error (SE)	Range %	Reduction of SE with each extra 100 in n
100	4.74	61.26 - 70.74	—
200	3.35	62.65 - 69.35	1.39
300	2.73	63.27 - 68.73	0.62
400	2.37	63.63 - 68.37	0.36
500	2.12	63.88 - 68.12	0.25
800	1.67	64.33 - 67.67	0.15(av.)
1000	1.50	64.50 - 67.50	0.12(av.)

This example shows two things that are always found in the relationship between sample size and standard error.

(1) To halve the standard error, the sample size must be increased fourfold.
(2) With each additional 100 in the sample size, the reduction in standard error is smaller (4th column).

Note The formula used here is —

Standard error of proportions $= \sqrt{\dfrac{(P \times Q)}{n}}$

where P = the percentage in favour
and Q = the balance (i.e. 100 - P)
and n = the size of the sample.

This formula is used on the assumption that each sample is a simple random sample. For other methods of sampling the formula would have to be modified.[3]

SAMPLE SIZE AND STANDARD ERROR
— when the expected majority opinion is likely to be
(1) overwhelming, say 92%
(2) marginal, say 52%
(3) as in the example on p. 113, 66%

Sample size (n)	(1)	(2)	(3)	(4)
100	2.71	5.00	4.74	4.61
200	1.92	3.53	3.35	3.18
300	1.57	2.88	2.73	2.52
400	1.36	2.50	2.37	2.12
500	1.21	2.23	2.12	1.83
800	0.96	1.77	1.67	1.30
1000	0.86	1.58	1.50	1.06

The figures for columns (1), (2), and (3) are without *finite population correction (fpc)*. Column (4) shows the effect of *fpc* applied to the 66 per cent case in column (3) when the total population is 2000.

Note that halving the standard error by quadrupling the sample size applies to the *uncorrected* standard errors, (1), (2), and (3). With *fpc* the same effect is achieved more economically, column (4).

The formula used here is the same as in the previous example on p. 113, but for column (4) the *fpc* is included thus:

$$\text{Standard error of proportions} = \sqrt{(1 - f)\frac{PQ}{n}}$$

Where f = the proportion included in the sample. For example, with a sample of 100 in 2000 the proportion is .05, and so on.

Probably no one needs to be convinced that the size of the sample is affected by: the level of accuracy required in the results; the variability of the population; the number of categories for analysis; the number of variables and questions; and the likely response rate. For those who are interested, there are also statistical formulae based on the way the estimated standard error is calculated.[4]

Much of the previous discussion, as we have seen, is based on the assumption that something is already known about the variability of the population, and the possible non-response rate. On these points and on many others a carefully conducted pilot survey is indispensable. If previous surveys do not provide any guide, then the pilot survey should. In any case the theoretically desirable size may be too large for the resources available for the survey. Shortage of money, time, and staff are likely to be the limiting factors. Probably the best advice is 'to take the largest sample financially possible *and* to discard questions for which a much larger sample would be needed to give useful results'[5]. It should be remembered however that a large sample is no guarantee that any differences between categories will be statistically significant; but it does increase the chances. Moreover a large non-random sample never compensates for faults in method: in fact size only accentuates any bias (the failure of the *Literary Digest* with its 10 million sample is a classic warning — see p. 92).

Let us suppose that nothing is known about the population to be surveyed — nothing, at least, that could help in predicting the size of sample needed. There are three pragmatic ways of handling this without stretching resources to the limit.

The method of serial groups is one method that will indicate when enough data have been collected. Returns for the first and second groups of, say, 100 (but it could be any number) are tabulated separately and compared. If statistical tests show that there are only small differences which are likely to have occurred by chance, then it is unnecessary to collect more data. In other words it must be shown statistically that the samples are similar but not just by chance. This is not the same as saying that there are no significant differences; with small samples important differences may fail to reach significant levels statistically just because the samples are too small.

Another criterion is when the difference between the two groups is less than the degree of error that can be tolerated. Let us suppose that a housing authority proposes to include a proportion of flats in a new tenancy housing development; and that they are prepared to risk disappointing no more than 10 per cent of their clients. Two random samples show that 62 per cent and 70 per cent of the potential tenants reject the idea of living in a flat (i.e. presumably between 38 per cent and 30 per cent would accept the offer of a flat).

On this basis it looks as though the average of 34 per cent would be the right proportion of flats to build and the risk of disappointing tenants would not be too high. But no account has been taken of sampling error. If the standard error for each sample is 5 per cent we can be fairly sure that the true proportions of those who would accept flats would be

1st sample 38 ± 5 per cent = 33 to 43 per cent
2nd sample 30 ± 5 per cent = 25 to 35 per cent

In other words the lowest estimate from the two samples would be 25 per cent and the highest 43 per cent and the authority can proceed to plan for 34 per cent of the new dwellings as flats. If the actual demand turns out to be high then 9 per cent of all clients will not be placed in the flats which they would have accepted; on the other hand, with a low demand for flats 9 per cent of the tenants will have to accept a flat unwillingly or go without. The sampling error in this example could be crucial. With a standard error of 6 per cent in each sample the possible range would increase by one at each end making it 24 to 44 per cent, so that 34 per cent could be exactly 10 per cent too much or too little; and a standard error of 7 per cent or more would widen the range still further with the consequent risk of exceeding the 10 per cent margin.

Providing the standard error is no more than 5 or 6 per cent (but only in this particular example), 34 per cent is the maximum proportion of flats that can be built within a 10 per cent margin of error. However the decision was based on a question that maximised *rejection* of flats: obviously by building fewer flats, the chances of disappointing less than 10 per cent would be much greater. But we must assume, for the purposes of this example, that the authority was trying to build as many flats as possible for financial reasons or for lack of space. The same procedure would work if the estimates were based on positive choice items such as 'Which house would you prefer — Type A or Type B?'

This procedure involves a high level of risk since it assumes that the two samples indicate the upper and lower limits of a potential preference. But this might not be so and the third or fourth sub-sample might fall outside this range. The method of 'cumulative frequency' meets this possibility. Like the method of serial groups this requires a short series of small samples. As the series proceeds, a cumulative percentage chart of the results is drawn. It would be reasonable to stop sampling at the point where the sampling error of the combined samples provides acceptable limits, or in other words, to stop when this sampling error is less than the degree of error that can be tolerated for practical purposes (as in the 'housing authority' example given previously).

In this whole discussion of sample size no account has been taken of the level of confidence required, though it has been mentioned. Confidence level will be discussed in the next chapter, under Inferential Statistics; meanwhile it can be noted that the standard error gives a margin of error or range which might be expected to hold for two out of every three samples (on average). If this level of confidence is not good enough or in other words the risk of being wrong is too high, then the margin of error could be based on *twice* the sampling error. This range would be expected to hold for as many as nineteen out of twenty or 95 per cent of similar random samples.

Thus, in the housing authority problem given above, further sampling would be necessary until the standard error could be reduced to 2½ per cent. We would then have a range of

34 ± 5 per cent (i.e. twice the standard error)

which could be expected for 95 per cent of similar random samples (or we could be wrong once in every twenty). This is more reassuring than the standard error of 5 per cent on a smaller sample that would have given the same range, 34 ± 5 per cent, but based on only one standard error and therefore likely to be wrong in one out of three cases.

However, these pragmatic methods must be used with caution and only when more precise predictions about sample size cannot be made. For those who want to use the more precise formulae there are many references at the end of this chapter.

Who is the right respondent?

When people have been selected by name there is no problem, though mistakes can occur if the interviewer fails to check that the person to be interviewed is actually the same as the one listed. But when houses or addresses have been selected without reference to individual names, the person who answers the door is not necessarily the person who has to be interviewed.

Kish[6] has provided a method that attempts to give all individuals in a household or dwelling an equal chance of selection. The system requires the interviewer to ask how many people aged 16 and over live at the address. Problems will arise if more than one household occupies the same address, but let us assume there is a single household. First all males and then all females are listed, both in descending order of age. These are numbered from 1 to 6 (or more). The person who is to be interviewed is selected by reference to the appropriate lines in a prepared selection table. Though the method does not ensure perfect equality of selection, it does avoid any bias effect due to interviewing only the person who answers the door.[7]

In some circumstances the survey results may need to be adjusted by weights according to the size of household, and the probability of selecting the household. But these are matters that are best discussed with a statistician should the need arise.

Not everybody who answers the door will help the interviewer draw up the preliminary list. As many as 2 per cent may refuse to do so; this would increase the non-response rate which is always a problem with any method of sampling.

The 'non-response' problem

The sampling frame may be nearly perfect and the sample may have been drawn according to all the rules for producing a probability or random sample. Much of this effort is wasted if the low response rate means that the actual sample bears little resemblance to the theoretical or target sample. People who are always out or do not reply are usually different in important respects from people who supply the data. If failure to reply occurred randomly over the sample then the replies obtained could be taken as representative of the whole intended sample. This is seldom the case and any gaps in the sample must be regarded as upsetting to some extent any random procedure.

Most social surveys have to face this problem but providing the non-response rate can be kept low and an estimate can be made of any sample bias, all is not lost. There are ways of doing both.

Not at home

People may be out when called on or they may be temporarily away from home, on holiday, in hospital or working elsewhere. If a specifically named person is required, rather than the current occupant, there is the further possibility that the person may have moved to a different address and it may not be possible to reach them. If the survey population is defined on the basis of residence, then the people who have moved may no longer be eligible for the sample.

In most cases, therefore, it is a question of calling back until contact is made. This will not apply to people whose temporary absence is longer than the survey period. A limit should be placed on the number of calls an interviewer may and must attempt before seeking a substitute or recording a final 'no contact' according to survey instructions. Re-calling adds to the survey costs but since the success rate tails off rapidly after the third or fourth call, the common practice is to require only two re-calls after the first call. In the United Kingdom, the Government Social Survey requires *at least* two re-calls and encourages more if success is in sight. Durbin and Stuart present evidence suggesting that two re-calls are more efficient than the method of unlimited re-calls. Besides the extra cost, later calls in their survey produced a rise in the refusal rate. They suggested that some interviewers may have entered 'refusals' at later calls to save them from making further calls[8]. In the Melbourne poverty survey up to eight calls were made in order to establish contact. All but 3.6 per cent were finally contacted.

There is also the problem of defining what constitutes a 're-call'. Obviously it is rather futile if the interviewer calls back after completing the other interviews in the street. Probably, calls at each address should be limited to one each morning, afternoon, and evening, that is if the interviewing must be completed in the one day. Otherwise it would be better to call back a day or two later, varying the part of the day in which the re-call is made.

In order to reduce the expense of calling back on all those who were out, one solution is to take a random sub-sample of them and to call back persistently, within reason, until an interview is obtained. However, it has been shown that the relative gain in efficiency is marginal as against the more usual method of calling back a specified number of times on everybody who is out the first time[9].

In mail surveys the method of interviewing a sub-sample of people who did not return the questionnaire does appear to be worthwhile[10]. In this case the questionnaire cannot be entirely anonymous though a separate name and address card or page can be returned with the questionnaire and separated before processing the replies. If this method is done systematically, the interview material is not simply pooled with the returns but is analysed separately. This gives an indication of the ways in which non-respondents differ from respondents. Expert statistical advice would be needed to determine the appropriate sub-sample ratio in relation to the extra cost of interviewing.

The Politz-Simmons method is another way of coping with the problem of people who are out when the interviewer calls. No re-calls are required. Allowance is made for the views and probable answers of those who are out on the basis of responses from those who are in but might have been out on another day. If the survey is taking place in the evenings, calls must be spread equally over the evenings of the week (usually excluding Sundays). Respondents are asked to say on how many of the five previous evenings (excluding Sunday) they would have been at home at about the time of the interview. A few may not give this extra information; in the Durbin and Stuart experiment, 5 per cent did not answer completely. If people are suspicious they might give misleading information, but refusing to answer would be the simple solution. Some dependence on the accuracy of recent memory is involved.

The probability of being found at home by the interviewer would range from one in six to six in six. The reciprocals of these probabilities are used as weights but the precise statistical procedures will be found in references given later.

From what has already been said about the possible differences between those who do and those who do not answer, it will be obvious that allowing interviewers to select substitutes is not really an answer to the problem. It certainly increases the sample size but does not reduce the risk of sample bias even if the substitutes are chosen by the same random procedure used for the survey. And this is the only acceptable method of permitting replacement by substitutes.

Reducing the number of refusals

Once the contact is made, very few people actually refuse to be interviewed: 5 per cent would be normal for general purpose surveys but the refusal rate could be higher for items concerning personal finance.

The experience and competence of the interviewer can decrease refusals.

If the sponsorship and purpose of the survey command respect, and if it is quite clear that no attempt will be made to sell anything or persuade the respondent to do anything other than answer a few questions, refusals will be minimal. The general approach of the interviewer should be warm and friendly and not overbearing; a genuine interest in other people helps. Even if the actual moment is not convenient for the respondent, an alternative time for the interview is often possible if the right approach is made. Experienced interviewers are therefore more successful than beginners. Whenever an interview was refused in the Melbourne poverty survey, another more experienced interviewer was sent out to make a further attempt. This resulted in a final refusal rate of less than 7 per cent in an obviously sensitive type of inquiry. Incidentally, the University of Melbourne's Institute of Applied Economic Research sponsored this 'Survey of Living Conditions in Melbourne'. An interviewer could hardly say that she had come to inquire about poverty!

Making prior appointments has succeeded in some investigations but failed in others. In our student surveys, appointments were made by telephone in nearly all cases, yielding response rates of around 98 per cent. In surveys of the general population, the use of the telephone could introduce sample bias. If the appointment is requested by letter, the usual high failure rate suffered by postal inquiries would apply. For some people, forewarned is forearmed, permitting escape. A prior personal call might just as well continue with the actual interview. Except in unusual kinds of survey, making prior appointments does not offer an infallible solution to the non-response problem.

If in spite of everything the desired respondent is still unwilling to be interviewed (and has not closed the door) it may be possible to arouse interest or curiosity with one well-chosen question. 'Perhaps, then, I could ask you just this: Do you think the town should grow rapidly, slowly, or stay the same size?' The interviewer then prepares to depart saying 'Well, that's the sort of thing I wanted to ask but I can see that you might prefer some other time.'

Allowing for non-response bias

In any case the interviewer should record as much as possible — sex, approximate age, any observable evidence that might indicate social class or even type of occupation, and the reason given for refusal. These details are essential for comparing refusers with respondents. With adequate information of this kind, supplemented if necessary by asking non-respondents of all types to return a card in a pre-paid envelope, it is possible to apply suitable statistical procedures adjusting the data to correct for any non-response bias in the survey.

Why me?

Finally, it is advisable to be prepared to explain why the person called for has been chosen for the survey. Perhaps it should be done in all cases. For many people 'chosen at random' means that anybody will do, and they might suggest trying someone else. The explanation needs to convey the idea that a proper cross-section of the population can only be obtained if the one in ten (or whatever ratio) selected at random are actually willing to answer the questions. And if the process selected a woman, then it is the woman and not her husband who should answer the questions.

Perhaps Coleridge should have the last word on sampling.

> 'It is an ancient Mariner,
> And he stoppeth one of three.
> "By thy long grey beard and glittering eye,
> Now wherefore stopp'st thou me?"'

(The Rime of the Ancient Mariner)

Notes

[1] G. Gardner, B.A. Sheil & V.A. Taylor, 'Passive politics: a survey of Melbourne University students', *Politics,* vol. V, no. 1, May 1970, pp. 30-7.

[2] Cantril, *op. cit.*

[3] See L. Kish, *Survey sampling,* Wiley, New York, 1965.

[4] Moser & Kalton, *op. cit.,* ch. 7.

[5] *ibid.,* p. 151.

[6] Kish, *op. cit.*

[7] *ibid.,* ch. 11 (pp. 396-404) contains a description of a technique for selecting persons from dwellings.

[8] Durbin & Stuart, *op. cit.,* p. 393.

[9] J. Durbin, 'Non-response and call-backs in surveys,' *Bulletin of the International Statistical Institute,* vol. 34, no. 2, 1954, pp. 72-86.

[10] P.G. Gray, 'A sample survey with both a postal and an interview stage', *Applied Statistics,* vol. 6, 1957, pp. 139-53.

Further reading

Much the same as for Chapter 8.

For sampling frame, size of sample, non-response problem, see Moser & Kalton, 1971, ch. 7.

On sample size: Cochran, 1963, ch. 4 ('The estimation of sample size') and Hansen *et al.,* 1953, pp. 126-31.

Imperfect sampling frames: Kish, 1965, ch. 11.

Non-sampling errors, response errors, etc.: Kish, 1965, ch. 13, and Moser & Kalton, 1971, ch. 15.

Chapter 10

What do the Results Say? Analysing and Interpreting Data

People are often tempted to see what they are looking for in the results. However if we want the truth and not merely comfortable confirmation of our own ideas, this temptation must be resisted. It is a fascinating sight to see an enthusiastic social scientist staring at a computer printout, or a table of results, and muttering 'Now what does this *tell* me?' We need to stand back from the results a little and let the data speak to us.

Understanding the results sometimes requires two separate processes. First, we must find out what the results are *saying* (descriptive analysis); then, and not before, we may search for what they *mean* (interpretation). An example will show that these are not the same thing.

Fictitious Table
Fertility and Age of Wife

	Wife's Age			
	20-29	30-39	40-49	50+
Average number of children reared	1.5	2.3	3.1	3.6

This table says that in a sample of wives in X-town (at a certain date), the average number of children they had reared or were rearing varied according to the wife's age in the manner shown. It does not say anything about the population of wives in the area from which the sample was drawn; to do so would require moving from a statistic based on a sample to a statement (really an estimate) about a parameter describing the survey population; such a statement would be the result of an inference. The table does not say anything about women in general since only wives are mentioned. It certainly does not say or mean that as wives get older they have more children. What does it mean? Without any other information it is difficult to interpret this table. It could mean, for instance, that families are getting smaller but since the women in the two lower age groups could presumably still have more children, this would be an unwarranted interpretation. In passing we might notice that the table itself can be criticised. 'Fertility' is not the same as 'number of children reared'; the table (and one might therefore assume the actual survey) makes no provision for wives under the age of twenty nor for unmarried mothers. The size of the sample is not given though this would not be unusual if details of the sample had been given in an earlier table.

Descriptive analysis is mainly a question of summarising in a suitable form the data we have collected. For this purpose we will probably use statistics for a quantitative description of the sample. However if we were describing a Youth Club or even comparing two Youth Clubs, we might do so in qualitative terms without the need to use any statistics.

There are two kinds of statistics used in analysis: **descriptive,** which have to come first, followed by **inferential** which are used for interpretation.

Descriptive statistics are used whenever you describe, in quantitative terms, your sample—or, if you have a complete census or enumeration, that is, a 100 per cent sample, your population. Descriptive statistics may be used even if the sample is not random. However, for inferential statistics, strictly speaking the sample must be random and preferably a probability sample. Inferential statistics are used whenever you wish to make statements about the population, that is, you infer that the population is like your sample. The inference will, of course, be in the form of an estimate, and is one form of interpretation.

The difficulty that arises from insistence on random samples for inferential statistics is that we often wish to interpret or explain data derived from non-random samples. The solution is to proceed with inferential statistics as if the samples were random, but to make it clear that they were not. Any subsequent conclusions must be regarded as tentative findings that are subject to the limitation that the samples were not in fact random or not completely random. This is quite fair when we remember that samples that were intended to be random and are treated as such, often fail to be completely random owing to non-response and other losses from the sample.

Examples of descriptive statistics

Basically these tell us how many there are of each kind of respondent, and how many said this or do that. These totals are known as statistical or frequency distributions or simply **frequencies** and are usually shown in the form of tables.

These tables may show the raw data (actual frequencies) or give the equivalent percentages. So long as the base line is given (the size of the sample), proportions or percentages help to provide a more readily understood picture. **Attributes** are usually handled in this way because subjects or units can only be classified and cannot be given a numerical score. This applies to such items as sex, marital status, and occupants (owner, tenant, lodger, and so on).

Variables, on the other hand, can be scored or scaled, making it possible to use averages; for example, items like age, rateable value, and distance from work. Simple descriptive measures can be used to give some indication of what might be regarded as 'typical'. Of the three **measures of central tendency** (the three Ms) — means (averages), medians, and modes — the mean would usually be chosen, but in some cases the median or the mode might be the more appropriate. For the grouped data of a variable, for example, ages 20-29, 30-39 and so on, percentages can also be used.

But how typical is the 'typical' value? The other scores may be very similar or very different, bunched together or spread evenly over the whole range. This can be seen in a graph though it might be necessary to arrange the scores in groups for convenience. The range of variation can also be indicated by one of the **measures of dispersion** such as the standard deviation which can easily be calculated. The actual range, from lowest to highest, requires no calculation, though the usefulness of the information is limited.

However these tables of gross totals cannot say very much — counting heads doesn't take us very far. We want to know what kinds of ideas are in which types of heads. In other words we wish to break down the totals into their component parts and analyse the data according to the various categories. These may include age, sex and occupation; in regional surveys, the district and size of town are usually important. The cross-classifications or cross-tabulations can be converted from table form to diagrams such as graphs and histograms.

Since the sub-groups are not likely to be the same size, it is necessary to convert the figures to a common base for comparison purposes. This can be done by using either proportions or percentages or by using a measure of **central tendency.**

Still at the descriptive level, though this is arguable, we might ask the data if there are any **relationships.** For example, are people who live in the outer suburbs more concerned about environmental problems than people who live in the inner suburbs? And is this attitude related to other factors such as social class? Trends of this sort might be discernible in the cross-tabulations but the strength of these relationships must be tested by calculating the correlation coefficients. For category-type data (attributes and grouped data) chi-squares might be more appropriate. On these points you will need to consult your friendly statistician.

At this point the distinction between descriptive analysis and interpretation becomes less sharp. One of my philosophy teachers, C. E. M. Joad, used to say that relationships cannot be observed, they can only be inferred. We can see the spade and we can see the ground; we *infer* that the spade is *in* the ground but the relationship itself ('in') cannot be observed.

If this argument applies to the analysis of research results, then it may be true that identifying relationships between variables is not purely descriptive, it is also inferential.

Examples of inferential statistics

There are two main purposes served by inferential statistics. The first is to relate the sample data to the population from which the sample is drawn. This is a process of **estimation** and involves the measurement of **standard errors** and **confidence levels.** The second is to test any apparent differences and relationships so that we can be reasonably sure that they did not show up by chance. This is a form of **hypothesis testing** and mainly involves significance tests such as 't' tests and contingency tests. Through inferential statistics we hope to move from description to interpretation or explanation.

Estimation

Unless we have made a complete enumeration, to infer that the population is like the sample always involves a certain amount of risk. With a probability sample we can calculate the sampling error or standard error which provides a basis for indicating the degree of risk. Non-probability samples provide no such basis and the risk is an uncertain amount. Strictly speaking, sampling errors and confidence limits cannot be estimated in quota sampling, for instance.

The standard error is really an estimate of the precision of a statistic such as the mean. If the mean age of a *sample* is 41 and the standard error is 1.25, the mean age of the *population* can be estimated as 41 ± 1.25 years. In other words the true mean age of the population is likely to be between 39.75 and 42.25 years. How sure can we be about this? If the population has a normal distribution of age (i.e., the curve of the frequency distribution would approximate a normal curve) then repeated random sampling with replacement would produce a mean within that range about 68 times out of 100 samples. This is known as the **confidence level.** We are saying in effect that there is a 68 per cent chance that the true mean age of the population is 41 ± 1.25 years. If this level of confidence is not good enough then we must extend the range and take twice the standard error. The fictitious example on p. 126 shows how this increases the confidence level or CL.

In other words the greater the range, the greater the cu..fidence level — as you would expect. Statistics are usually quoted with one standard error thus, 41 ± 1.25 years.

**Estimated Range of Mean Age related to
Confidence Level — when the Standard
Error (SE) is 1.25 years**

Age	Range	CL
41 ± 1(SE)	39.75 - 42.25	68%
41 ± 2(SE)	38.50 - 43.50	95%
41 ± 3(SE)	37.25 - 44.75	99%

In practice the 95 per cent confidence level is usually reversed and stated in terms of probability, thus $p = \cdot 05$. This is often referred to as the 5 per cent level of confidence meaning 'I could be wrong five times out of a hundred'. When it comes to making statements about differences between means or correlation coefficients, social scientists prefer to be on the safe side. They accept as statistically significant only those differences that could not have occurred by chance more than five times out of a hundred. In probability terms p must be equal to or less than $\cdot 05$.

Hypothesis testing

The hypothesis to be tested may be that men are different from women! More specifically we may wish to know whether their opinions differ.
  Take the following example (adapted from Moser & Kalton, p. 75):

Sample	*Result*
400 men	52% in favour of flats
400 women	45% in favour of flats

We are not immediately entitled to conclude that men are more favourable than women. The difference must first be tested. If the difference is no larger than can be expected by chance due to the fact that these are samples, then we must conclude that there is possibly no real difference. Or, as the statistician would say, we cannot reject the null hypothesis that there is *no* difference since the difference is not statistically significant.
  There are statistical methods of testing differences, known as **significance tests**[1]. For the example above, Moser and Kalton tested the difference between the two sample proportions and found that it was large enough to be acceptable at the 5 per cent level of confidence. This does not mean that you can always accept a 52-45 per cent difference or any 7 per cent difference as significant. It would depend on the size of the samples.
  Significance tests can also be applied to correlation coefficients and to the difference between correlations. (see p. 128.)

The hypotheses to be tested may be formulated before you collect the data or after you look at the results. Hypotheses made before the survey are in fact predictions and may be of two kinds.

(a) You predict that the results will go in one direction rather than another (for example that men will be more favourable than women to a specified planning proposal). The appropriate test of the significance of the difference will be a 'one-tail' test.

(b) If there are no grounds for saying which way the difference will go, the hypothesis becomes a prediction that there will be no difference; there is no point in predicting a difference if you cannot say which way it will go though you still might expect to find a difference. In any case the appropriate test is one that tests the proposition that there is no difference and this requires a 'two-tail' test. The level of confidence resulting from a two-tail test is lower than that given by a one-tail test. For this reason researchers prefer to make uni-directional predictions if possible rather than predictions that could be right or wrong in two different directions.

Propositions made after inspecting the results, whether or not they state the direction of any differences, are not predictions. Any tests of these hypotheses must be regarded as a form of exploratory analysis for which two-tail tests of significance are required.

Estimation and hypothesis testing both require descriptive statistics as a basis; inferential statistics are needed to complete each process.

To recapitulate: the task of analysis and interpretation can be seen as an attempt to answer two questions: What do the results say? and What do the results mean?

Description is an account of what the results say and for this purpose we use descriptive statistics. This description refers originally to the sample but by using inferential statistics we can make statements in the form of estimates about the population that the sample is supposed to represent. By inference we are able to describe the population in the same terms as those used to describe the sample.

In each case, whether we are describing the sample directly or the population by inference, it can be done in two ways.

Numerative: one variable at a time (frequencies, proportions, central tendencies, etc.)

Comparative: two or more variables, usually by comparing two at a time, or one series with another as in the fictitious table at the beginning of this chapter.

Hypothesis testing is a form of testing these comparisons; the hypotheses may be precise predictions before the results are in, or they may be exploratory hypotheses either before or after seeing the results. This difference affects the ensuing level of confidence; we have more confidence in predictions that are confirmed than in differences that are · discovered.

Perhaps our curiosity will come to rest at this point. But we may wish to go on with a further question: How can the results be explained?

Explanation: This may be regarded as interpretation at a higher level and possibly more satisfying for the researcher. But it is more difficult and there are many pitfalls. Many fools rush in where statisticians (who may not be angels) fear to tread.

Take for example the case of a correlation. The results are saying that two things go together or are related in some way, in terms of the measurements used. The **correlation coefficient** (a descriptive statistic) estimates the strength of this relationship. Is it a case of cause and effect, like the interpretation of the established correlation between smoking and lung cancer, or is some other explanation possible? Unfortunately a single survey is rarely able to supply data that can unequivocally yield a causal explanation. The best one can do is to put forward plausible explanations that are at least consistent with the data.

Given that a correlation coefficient is found to be significant at the 1 per cent or 5 per cent level of confidence, what does this mean? In the first place it means that the relationship is probably a true description of the attributes or variables and is not one that is likely to occur by chance more than once (1 per cent) or five times (5 per cent) in one hundred similar samples. Here, 'similar' means 'drawn by the same random method from the same original population (with replacement, i.e. the units drawn in one sampling are returned to the pool or sampling frame)'. In other words, we can confidently assume that the two variables are related in some way. But how?

The relationship need not be a simple case of cause and effect; there may be a common 'cause' or determinant of both. If there is a correlation of ± 0.75 with $p < .01$ between factors A and B, then

1. A may be a cause of B
2. B may be a cause of A
3. A and B may affect each other
4. A and B may both depend on or be affected by X which may at this stage be an unknown factor.

The statements that suggest that 'A is the cause of B' must not be taken literally because B may have existed regardless of A. Statements of causal direction (A causes B, and so on) are meant to be interpreted as effect statements, that is, A has an effect on B.

Given a correlation between two factors, with the possibility of a causal link with a third factor, there are fifty-six different possible causal interpretations (see Appendix A). This shows how careful one must be before assuming that the obvious interpretation is necessarily the correct or only one.

A simple example will illustrate some of the possibilities. Ecological studies of the incidence of schizophrenia have shown that this mental disorder occurs disproportionately more in economically depressed areas[2]. In other words higher ratios of schizophrenia per head occur in these sub-standard areas (previously called 'slums'). Between these two factors alone there are four possible direct causal relationships.

(1) Living in a depressed area (DA) is more likely to make people become schizophrenic (S).

$$DA \rightarrow S$$

(2) Having a high proportion of schizophrenics in the population depresses the area.

$$S \rightarrow DA$$

(3) Schizophrenics are unable to keep a steady job, become hard up and gravitate towards cheap rent areas.

$$\text{again } S \rightarrow DA$$

Notice that (2) and (3) could both be true at the same time; and one or both could be true at the same time as (1), hence —

(4) Schizophrenia and poor housing (DA) reinforce each other, so that as one increases it helps to increase the other.

$$S \rightleftarrows DA$$

So far nothing has been said about the possibility of these two factors being the result of a common origin or cause, namely heredity or genetic factors (GF). This would be (5)

$$DA \overset{GF}{\underset{}{\nearrow \searrow}} S$$

and the correlation between DA and S would not necessarily mean that there was any direct causal relationship between them.

Are there any other possibilities? Theoretically there are, though in this example it would be necessary to stretch the imagination. For example the third factor might be a common link or mediating factor. Suppose that it is 'loss of friendship', then we might have

(6) Schizophrenia leads to loss of friendship (LF), which leads to (a) domestic neglect (and so on to DA); or (b) seeking friends by going to live in depressed areas.

$$S \rightarrow LF \rightarrow DA$$

And of course another possibility would be

(7) $$DA \rightarrow LF \rightarrow S$$

There seem to be no end to the possible combinations (though I think that fifty-six is about the limit). For instance —

(8) $$S \rightleftarrows LF \rightarrow DA$$
(9) $$DA \rightleftarrows LF \rightarrow S$$
(10) $$DA \rightleftarrows LF \rightleftarrows S$$

In Australia, as in the United Kingdom, Israel, and USA, migrants from many lands tend to live in national groups in different localities. This may simply be due to the operation of friendship and family ties. But are other explanations possible? We would have to exclude on logical grounds the possibility that living in an Italian area could change a person into an Italian immigrant. But who knows?

Common sense can help us to eliminate some theoretically possible causal explanations for a correlation between two variables. There is probably a strong correlation between watching TV (total man-hours) and the weather (temperature and/or rainfall) but it would be ludicrous to suggest that our watching TV affects the weather. Similarly, age is often found to be associated with education, income, political and social attitudes. For instance older people are more conservative than younger people but one can hardly imagine that becoming more conservative in outlook increases a person's chronological age. But as the other variables are also correlated, several other kinds of causal links are theoretically possible.

Some of these can be tested by the method of **partial correlation.** This is a method for eliminating the effects of one variable upon the relation between two other variables. We discover what happens to the correlation between two variables when a third (say, age) is held constant (age not allowed to vary while we look at the other two variables). If within age groups the correlation between income and conservatism disappears, then age is the common factor that affects both income and conservatism and could account for the apparent relation between them. But if the correlation persists, then other possibilities cannot be rejected. For example, perhaps age increases income which in turn increases conservatism. The possibility that by or after becoming more conservative people may increase their incomes (say through promotion or changing to more profitable forms of private enterprise) still remains to be tested.

Surveys usually produce cross-sectional data at a given point in time, even though the actual data gathering may extend over many days or weeks. Long-term or longitudinal studies involve special difficulties such as contacting the original respondents again after a suitable interval. Many may have moved away or died. The Department of Psychology at the University of Melbourne has been conducting such a follow-up study since 1957 when 392 boys were interviewed; ten years later, 356 of these boys, now men of course, were re-interviewed. This is a re-interview rate of 91 per cent and I doubt if any other study has ever achieved more than this after a ten-year interval. The analysis is proceeding but some aspects have already been reported.[3]

Longitudinal studies can be done in two ways.

1. Panel design — re-questioning the same people after a reasonable interval or at intervals. Confidentiality can be assured, but not anonymity. Variations of this design include sub-sampling so that one set is re-questioned after the first interval and another after the second interval and so on. Some sets may be re-questioned more than once during the whole period.

2. Matched samples design. This avoids re-questioning the same

people. Hence it avoids any triggering effect that may stimulate interests and activities between one interview and the next. Not entirely, perhaps, because respondents in the first sample may talk to others afterwards and this 'leakage' could seep into a second sample. The method has many advantages but no matching of samples can ever be as perfect as matching an individual with himself.

The point of this digressive discussion or discursion into survey method is that, strictly speaking, longitudinal effects can only be claimed on the basis of longitudinal studies. It is an error of interpretation to deduce longitudinal effects on the basis of one cross-sectional survey without any further evidence.

Take for example cross-sectional data showing that the older age groups have higher percentages of 'conservatives' than lower age groups. Does this mean that people become more conservative as they get older? This would be assuming a longitudinal effect without further evidence. In fact the people in the older age groups may have been just as conservative when they were twenty or thirty.

It is probably true that the public now have higher expectations regarding hospitals than in previous decades. Lyons[4] found that hospital patients over the age of forty were more satisfied with hospital treatment and conditions in the wards than the patients who were under forty.

It would be tempting to interpret this as indicating that the increase in public expectations applies more to younger people than to those over forty. The results might also be claimed as supporting the notion that young people are becoming more questioning and less accepting of social values and standards than their parents. Perhaps this is what we want to believe and we may see in the results what we are looking for. But how do we know what these older people expected and accepted when they were younger?

On the basis of cross-sectional data alone, we cannot assume that people become more conservative as they grow older, nor that people who are satisfied with life today were just as satisfied with life when they were young.

The so-called generation gap is another example of hasty interpretation of inadequate cross-sectional data. This comes from comparing young people in general with older people in general, instead of comparing young people with their own parents. In Melbourne, it was found that as regards religion and politics, students were remarkably like their parents.[5] However it is possible that this similarity of attitude holds only when parents and their children have a similar educational background. Differences occur between generations and also within generations when educational levels are compared. It is also an educational gap and any apparent generation gap is partly dependent upon educational differences.

This last example illustrates the danger of interpreting a relationship between two variables (age and attitudes) without considering any others such as education, social class, occupation and so on. Social scientists are increasingly turning to multivariate survey designs especially now that more sophisticated forms of statistical analysis are available. The days have long since gone when a student would be expected to vary one thing at a time and observe how variations in one factor (the **independent variable**) affected the operation of another factor (the **dependent variable**).

But the complexities of interpreting multivariate relationships obtained in the analysis of survey data are beyond the scope of this book. The use of partial correlations and regressions already suggested would be one, relatively simple, step. But to develop more precise causal models to explain the data, though very exciting, is full of traps for the inexperienced investigator — and sometimes for the experienced one too. The intrepid student may need some of the references given at the end of this chapter — or have to consult a statistician on the mysteries of linkage analysis, causal path analysis and the like.

One other problem remains and that is the danger of using too many tests of significance. This will not happen if the survey has been designed carefully and parsimoniously. But as most surveys now go through a computer there is a temptation to put everything in without attempting to be selective. 'Why worry?' is the attitude of some enthusiasts. 'Let's ask as many questions as we can, put it all through the computer and see what happens.' Computer programs are available to carry out advanced multivariate analyses and do all the tests of significance that are possible. This is the trap. Out of one hundred tests of significance carried out on the same sample, five results will (on average) be significant at the 5 per cent level of confidence *by chance* (including one at $p = .01$). Hence the danger of selecting as truly significant only those results that were wanted. If there are just ten significant results, five could have reached the 5 per cent level by chance. On what grounds can it be said that the five that are interesting are the significant results and the remainder are the chance results to be discarded? Could it not have been the other way round? I recently read a survey report in which the author had faithfully but foolishly reported the results of all the 36 000 tests of significance churned out by the computer.

There is no clear-cut statistical answer, and interpretation may border on the subjective. If among the significant results there is a sub-set that makes sense, then they can be accepted. There may be more than one of these logical sub-sets patterns. Anything else must be regarded as interesting but enigmatic and firmly discarded unless it can be seen as fitting into an alternative pattern.

Two other solutions are possible.

1. To accept all the results on the understanding that the survey is purely exploratory. This means using the survey as a method of discovery

and not a method of proof (adopting J. S. Mill's terminology). Any attempt at proof would require a separate exercise, specially designed for the purpose, at a subsequent date when some factors may have undergone change.

2. To specify in advance which sub-set of results will be considered relevant. The analysis is limited to these, while the rest remain in cold storage, tempting but untouchable. After, and only after, the main analysis has been completed and written up (if not publicly reported), the cold storage may be converted into a goldfield and the explorer may fossick for interesting discoveries to be used as the basis for further research.

Another remedy for this excess of results may be adopted. The survey analyst takes a more stringent level of confidence, say p equal to or less than .01 or even $p = .001$. But, depending on the total number of tests or population of results, the same problem exists in principle though there are fewer significant results competing for acceptance. It takes a strong determination or courage (perhaps even self-sacrifice) to limit oneself in this way and to ignore results that might otherwise have been regarded as 'interesting'.

The moral is that in planning the survey it is wise to be cautious and aim for a limited number of specific objectives. Otherwise the researcher can be carried away by the temptation to leave everything to the computer.

Notes

[1]See J. Lumsden, *Elementary statistical method*, University of Western Australia Press, Nedlands, 1969, pp. 83-106; also Moser & Kalton, *op. cit.*, pp. 74-6, 151-2, 444-47.

[2]See J.A. Clausen & M.L. Kohn, 'The ecological approach in social psychiatry', in N.J. Smelser & W.T. Smelser (eds), *Personality and social systems*, Wiley, New York, 1963, pp. 87-100.

[3]S.B. Hammond, *Boy and man*, mimeo, Department of Psychology, University of Melbourne, 1974.

[4]R. Lyons, *Patient attitudes toward the Preston and Northcote Community Hospital*, unpublished M. Sc. thesis in Occupational Psychology, University of Melbourne, 1974.

[5]G. Gardner, *Student demonstrators at Melbourne University*, Paper presented at the Sixth Annual Conference of the Australian Psychological Society, Melbourne, August 1971.

Further reading

On statistical inference see Kish, 1965, pp. 14-17 and ch. 14.

Chapters on the analysis of data are to be found in: Goode & Hatt, 1952; Moser & Kalton, 1971; Selltiz *et al.,* 1960; and Stacey, 1969.

If you are particularly interested in multivariate analysis and the interpretation of correlations, read: Blalock, 1964; Hyman, 1955; and Kerlinger & Pedhazur, 1973 (pp. 305-33 for section on path analysis). As Kerlinger & Pedhazur emphasise: 'path analysis is not a method for discovering causes' (p. 305) but a method of testing theories about the direction of causation between variables.

Chapter 11

Writing Survey Reports

'Research not reported is research not done.' Whoever first said this may not have known how difficult it could be and how long it could take to get a research report published. Perhaps there were fewer difficulties and shorter time lags when the aphorism was first made.[1]

Not everything deserves to be published of course, and in any case some surveys are confidential to the client or organisation concerned. But unless the survey has been written up and a report made available, whether privately or publicly, one might as well acknowledge that the research is incomplete. Apart from the experience gained by those who took part, there is nothing to show for the work done.

The format, contents and style of the report will depend upon who is intended to be the reader. Clients are usually less interested in details and problems of method, statistical procedures, and theoretical issues; they look for a precise statement of the conclusions reached, without too many reservations, and often expect to find recommendations. A more scientific approach will be required for an academic or professional journal, with clear descriptions of method and evidence relating to accuracy and confidence levels. For the popular press and for special interest journals such as those on management or the environment, the message will have to be clear and crisp. Owing to limitations of space the writer will often be seen as claiming more and expressing greater certainty than his normal caution would permit.

Survey reports usually follow the logical sequence regarded as suitable for technical reports and academic theses. It is difficult to vary this sequence without putting the cart before the horse. However, reports intended for boards of directors or high-ranking officials of local authorities will often begin with conclusions or even recommendations. Unless these busy people are convinced that some practical outcome is possible, they are not likely to waste time reading something on the off-chance that it may be interesting.

The first section or **introduction** explains *why* the survey was done; the **method**, which follows, shows *how* it was done. The **results** found and the

conclusions drawn then logically follow. Finally there is often a **discussion** section. This is the sequence expected in most universities and usually followed by professional agencies. Dr Buzzard, who was for many years Director of the National Institute of Industrial Psychology in London, favoured this sequence in the notes he wrote for the guidance of the staff (see below). The same format is often followed in journals, or in research reports with limited distribution as for example when the report is printed or duplicated by the department in which the work was done and is available on application to the author or the department.

THE BASIC STRUCTURE OF A REPORT
(According to R.B. Buzzard[2])

Purpose or object: what you set out to do
Methods: how you went about it
Results: what you found
Conclusions: what follows from the results

The following two further sections can be added if appropriate.

Discussion: what you thought about it all
Recommendations: what you think ought to be
                 done about it

The headings may be varied.

The introduction gives the general background to the problem or of the subject to be investigated. Relevant studies are discussed or sometimes cited as evidence. Within this general review specific problems are given special attention with more detailed discussion of reported findings in the literature. This leads to a statement of the purpose of the survey with perhaps a precise formulation of the hypotheses to be tested; but if the survey is exploratory then this should be made clear. Statistical inference procedures allow more confidence in the result that was predicted than in the same statistical result that either was not or could not have been predicted.

The method section explains the general design of the survey and gives reasons for the choice of methods. The survey population is defined, sampling ratios stated, and the suitability of the sampling frame and sampling method discussed. The size of the actual sample may be included, though this will be repeated when the details are given under results.

The procedure for arriving at the final choice of questions is described, with examples and reasons for key questions. The full questionnaire may be included as an appendix to the report rather than take up too much space in the text. Similarly, details of any interview procedure, the method and extent of interviewer training, and field procedures in general may be mentioned briefly in this section but with fuller details in an appendix.

In addition to describing how the required information is going to be obtained, it is usual to state how the data will be analysed and what statistical procedures will be used. If tests of significance are going to be used, they are specified and a statement is made as to the level of confidence which will be accepted.

There is some flexibility in the sequence of sub-sections. When appropriate the survey population may be described in the introduction. Also, some writers prefer to wait until the results section before stating the method of analysis and significance decision rules.

In the section on results, details of the sample should be reported, including —

    (a) total number in the intended sample,
    (b) total number contacted,
    (c) total number of actual respondents,
    (d) total number of usable respondents.

These figures are best given in tables, showing different categories (say, male and female, or whatever is appropriate) for each total. Percentages should be given for each sub-total; these make it evident whether it has been harder to contact one category than another and whether response rates and usable rates differ for the two categories. The significance or non-significance of any differences must be reported.

The non-response rate is the percentage difference between (a) and (c) and is made up of the sample units not contacted, and those that refused to reply (or to be interviewed).

In some cases a returned questionnaire may be unusable because vital personal or profile information may be missing or too many replies may be impossible to code. There will often be some items for which the data will be missing, but if the gaps are not vital or too many, the rest of the items can still be usable.

It is useful to give the actual response rate, i.e. $\frac{c}{a} \times 100$ (providing unusable returns are not a serious problem), as well as the refusal rate, which is $\frac{b-c}{b} \times 100$. The refusal rate indicates to what extent people were unwilling to answer, although contacted. This is distinct from the actual response rate, which shows how successful the survey was in contacting and questioning the sample units. The report should give the main reasons for failure to contact and, if known, the reasons for refusing to reply — with the frequencies in each case.

The writer should then state on what basis the effective sample (usable data) can be regarded as representative of the survey population. Alternatively it must be argued that the sample obtained is as representative as can be expected in the circumstances. If there are doubts about this, then the report should say so and advise special caution in interpreting the results which follow.

The results should also be presented in the form of tables, each one preceded by a brief introduction and followed by an equally brief comment. Discussion is usually deferred to the next section. The title of each table should be self-explanatory as far as possible and appear at top, whereas the titles of graphs and figures go beneath. The mnemonic is —

> Titles
> Tables — at top
> Figures — at foot

though any logic for this convention is not apparent.

As Buzzard (1972) says: 'Results are not conclusions.' Following the distinction made in the previous chapter, results are obtained by *analysing* the data; conclusions are made by *interpreting* the results.

There are two kinds of conclusions. Let us call them first and second order conclusions respectively. First-order conclusions are verbal or symbolic statements about numerical results; for example, the women of Eckstown are more concerned than the men about inadequate public transport services. Second-order conclusions usually follow some discussion and are the decisions the author wishes to make on the basis of his findings. For example, he may decide that the reasons for the women's greater concern (if these were not explored directly in the survey) can be deduced by reference to other data in the survey (such as location of shops,) or on the basis of some other knowledge about the district, or by speculation. Other second-order conclusions might be that the survey itself was inadequate, or that further investigations are necessary, or that the proposed new shopping centre will increase (or decrease) concern about public transport. Any prediction must of necessity be a second-order conclusion; predictions coming out of social surveys are based on first-order conclusions about the data.

Some brief discussion is permitted in the results section. It is not easy nor indeed necessary to delay any discussion until a later section. News and views may be interwoven providing they are separately identifiable. In other words results and first-order conclusions ('news') must stick closely to the facts, whereas discussion and second-order conclusions ('views') may involve opinion, imagination, prediction, and a synthesis that goes beyond the reported data. Sometimes it will be appropriate to state an opinion at the point where the result is reported, but in general the author should save 'views' for the discussion section.

The discussion section attempts to make sense of the results and bring out any underlying consistency or pattern in the separate results. Definitive interpretations must not go beyond the results obtained, but speculative interpretation is permissible and often desirable providing it is made quite clear that the case is being argued on grounds other than the actual evidence in the survey. Comparisons with other surveys and research findings should be made, emphasising any similarities and differences.

Inconsistencies within the results, or between the results and others previously reported, should be discussed and likely explanations developed.

The results may fail to support hypotheses or expectations either by not reaching an acceptable level of significance or by contradicting the predictions. In such cases the report writer has two options. He can question the theory or the deductions on which the predictions were made: for some reason what was found in another place does not apply to the survey population chosen. Perhaps he can suggest some other factors, which should have been taken into account. Alternatively, (though it may be additionally) the methods he used may not have been appropriate, or did not work. Improvements, different designs and techniques, perhaps different or re-worded questions can be discussed.

In fact it often seems that there is more to write about if the results are negative, disappointing, or in some way contradictory, than if they are confirmatory. Contradictions have to be explained, and further research into the contradictions and the exceptional cases can often yield important new insights. What can you say about confirmatory results other than 'I told you so'?

Though it may be harder to discuss the survey that turned out as expected, we can again do so in terms of theory and method; but in this case it seems appropriate to take questions of method first. As far as can be seen, the method worked but this is no excuse for complacency. Could a different design and other techniques, or improved items, sharpen still further the differences that were found and the similarities? Were the results merely a reflection of the methods used? Given the situation and the techniques, and the questions selected, could the survey have produced anything else? No method is perfect if the survey made it impossible for some people to reveal their true attitudes. Having satisfied any doubts on these points, the report can turn to the theoretical implications of the findings. Perhaps these tend to support one theory more than another.

If either case, whether the results provide confirmation or not, the report can end with some indication of the direction future surveys should take and also make specific suggestions for further investigations. Implications for policy decisions can be suggested. Depending on the purpose of the report, some recommendations may be included which appear to follow from the findings of the survey. For example, a few were made at the end of the book reporting the survey on people in poverty in Melbourne.[3]

There should be an overall logical unity and sequence apparent in the presentation of a report. The purpose of the survey should be justifiable;

hypotheses and predictions should follow logically from the introduction. It should be clear that the methods are appropriate for the purpose and that the items chosen will in fact provide the information necessary to test the predictions or explore the relevant material. The results that are reported should be relevant to the ideas put forward in the introduction and probably follow a similar sequence; the conclusions should be literate, but logical, statements of the numerical facts. Unexpected findings should normally be reported after the main objectives have been satisfied. However, if the surprise element affects the whole interpretation of the results, then logically it should precede them. Finally, the discussion should be a logical development of the results and be closely related to them. The informed researcher has the right (some would say the duty) to speculate beyond the narrow limits of the results, using any insights he has gained in the course of the survey or previously. But these speculations must be logically valid even though they are put forward tentatively. The report must not go beyond the results and claim more than they reveal.

A full report in the form detailed above would amount to something like a university thesis for a higher degree. Most reports would be much shorter, depending on the purpose of the report. The author must decide how much introduction the reader requires in order to understand why the survey was done. In some cases hardly any introduction might be needed. If there has been very little work previously reported on, say, the special housing requirements of elderly people, then it could be fairly obvious that it was time some information was gathered on this question.

In other cases there may be an extensive literature, and even rival theories that could lead to conflicting predictions. Much has been written, for instance, about the attitudes of workers to their jobs, and how these attitudes are related in one way to matters inside the factory (methods of supervision, technology and so on) and in another way to external social forces. Different theories would justify quite different predictions as to the outcome of a comparison between assembly-line workers and automated-production workers. Vaughan[4] chose the occasion of a strike in a Melbourne car factory to make this comparison and test certain predictions. The report on the ensuing survey contains enough theoretical discussion to clarify the purpose of the survey.

The length of the section on method will vary depending on the complexity of the procedures used and whether there is any need to justify using one method rather than another. Similarly the writer may be reporting all his numerous results or just one of them and the conclusions may be straightforward or highly contentious.

Margaret Stacey[5] has listed a dozen minimum items to include in a social research report. These form a most useful check-list.

The sequence described in this chapter may need to be changed for some forms of reporting. Some technical reports and commissioned reports may begin with a short summary or abstract. They may then immediately list the conclusions and recommendations (if any) before going on to describe the rationale, methods, and results. More popular accounts for the press or special interest journals may begin with an attention-snatching statement of a somewhat startling result. Supporting information may then follow and will often be inadequate for the intelligent reader who wants to know more about method and results before assessing the accuracy of the report.

MINIMUM ITEMS TO INCLUDE IN A SOCIAL RESEARCH REPORT
(According to Margaret Stacey[6])

1. By whom, for whom, and with what financial backing the research was undertaken.
2. The objects of the research.
3. The time at which the field work was undertaken and its duration
4. The universe which was the subject of the research, including basic demographic details.
5. The details of any samples taken which should include: the size of the sample; the sample fraction; the method of sampling; the number of completed interviews related to the number of planned interviews.
6. Descriptions of the methods of data collection: whether from documents, observation, or interview and the type of each used.
7. Details of the staff employed and their supervision.
8. A copy of any questionnaires, schedules, or interview guides used.
9. The facts found, including those contrary to the hypotheses.
10. Where data is [sic] presented in the form of percentages or other indices, tables should include the number of cases on which these were based.
11. The relation of the evidence collected to comparable information collected in other studies.
12. As appropriate, the implications of the findings for previously stated theoretical propositions and/or for action.

So far nothing has been said about style of writing. Anyone who has not browsed through Gowers[7] will inevitably fall into one of the many traps set for unwary writers. (And I do mean 'browsed', having just looked it up to make sure: it means, figuratively, to read for enjoyment.) Though style may inevitably reflect some characteristics of the writer, there are some basic rules that help communication. Obviously jargon should be avoided; simple words and phrases should be used unless they happen to be misleading or possibly inaccurate. The term 'male subjects' is sometimes more accurate than the term 'men'; and 'persons aged 40 years and over' is more precise than 'people over the age of forty'. If technical terms are unavoidable they should be explained.

Long, involved sentences tend to be confusing, especially when the subject of the sentence becomes separated from its verb by many qualifying clauses. (I could have written: 'Long, involved sentences, which some people, bent on impressing their public, seem to enjoy writing even though the subject of the sentence, in far too many cases to permit ease of comprehension, becomes separated from its verb by many qualifying clauses, tend to become confusing.')

On the other hand, though short sentences are desirable, too many in quick succession can be monotonous. Sentence length needs to be varied.

'If you can't say it simply, simply don't say it' is good advice in principle, but there are times when one must persist in saying something that cannot be said simply, because the matter itself is complex. Some of you may have found that the chapters on sampling, and my attempts to explain statistical concepts, lacked simplicity at times. But in these matters over-simplification can be misleading too and I suspect that even my friendly statistician would frown at some of my attempts.

There are, of course, some people who are never impressed if they find that they can understand every word. It can't be deep enough for them if they were never in danger of drowning. But the purpose of a survey report is to communicate, and perhaps to impress by competence rather than by obscurity.

Finally, you may need to list the sources of your information and the publications or other material that you have found useful. List them alphabetically under authors' names in a section called 'References', and not as a bibliography. Do not include anything that you have not at least partly read (for example, even if you have read only the relevant chapter, you may list the book title). A bibliography is a list of reading material with the implication that it either includes everything worth reading on the subject or is a suitable selection. It may be appropriate to include a bibliography at the end of a book; it is rarely appropriate to include one at the end of a survey report.[8]

Notes

[1]'The research task is not completed until the report has been written'. This is how the point is made by Selltiz *et al., op. cit.,* p. 442. See also their ch. 12 'The research report', for further guidance on writing reports.

[2]From R.B. Buzzard, 'Notes on report writing', *Occupational Psychology,* vol. 46, 1972, pp. 201-7. This article is based on notes Dr Buzzard wrote for the guidance of the research staff of the National Institute of Industrial Psychology, London, when he was Director.

[3]Henderson *et al., op. cit.*

[4]E.J. Vaughan, *Perception of work among factory workers,* unpublished MA thesis, University of Melbourne, 1974.

[5]M. Stacey, *Methods of social research,* Pergamon Press, Oxford, 1969.

[6]*ibid.,* pp. 143-4. Margaret Stacey acknowledges that in drawing up the list she was 'guided particularly by The Market Research Society, *Standards in market research,* Part IV Standards, in reporting on sample surveys, London, 1965, and by the National Institute for Social Work Training, *Research in the personal social services: Proposals for a Code of Practice*, National Council of Social Service, London, 1965'.

[7]E. Gowers, *The complete plain words*, Penguin, Harmondsworth, 1974.

[8]See J. Barzun & H.F. Graff, *The modern researcher*, Harcourt, Brace & World, New York, rev. edn, 1970. The book is written mainly for historians rather than social historians, which in a sense is what we are when we carry out social surveys. Part Three is on 'Writing', and as the following chapter headings show, is full of relevant advice for anyone writing a research or survey report.

Chapter 11   Organising: Paragraph, Chapter, and Part
Chapter 12   Plain Words: The War on Jargon and Clichés
Chapter 13   Clear Sentences: Right Emphasis and Right Rhythm
Chapter 14   The Arts of Quoting and Translating
Chapter 15   The Rules of Citing: Footnotes and Bibliography
Chapter 16   Revising for Printer and Public

Further reading

Gowers, 1974; Barzun & Graff, 1970; Selltiz *et al.,* 1960, ch. 12.

Chapter 12

Criticisms of Social Surveys

Social scientists love arguing. It might seem that there is no point in arguing about social surveys as a method; some people find them useful, others do not. The merits of a particular survey can be questioned according to whether it violates or satisfies some of the principles described in this book and elsewhere. In addition there are numerous discussions about the merits of particular techniques used in surveys. Interviews can be compared with mail questionnaires, as in Chapter 7. Some survey practitioners do not approve of quota sampling for reasons given in Chapter 8. Often the issue concerns the relative efficiency of different techniques, the best way of getting high response rates, and such minute details as the optimum number of times an interviewer should call back in order to obtain an interview. These disputes can be settled, for the time being, by empirical evidence; experimental surveys can be designed to provide comparative data; when finance is restricted, a cost-benefit analysis may help.

The issues that will be outlined in this chapter are not like this; instead they usually involve an element that is outside empirical inquiry. For some issues, data may be relevant and useful in disclosing effects without helping us to decide if these effects are desirable. For instance, whether social surveys arouse or change attitudes, or fail to evoke any active interest, is an empirical question on which data could be helpful. But whether it is *ethical* to arouse or change attitudes, or fail to evoke any social response is a different matter; one that cannot be decided by data. Other issues are about ultimate values and give rise to 'pure' arguments that cannot be 'contaminated' by data. However I could be wrong about this. Someone may devise ways of settling these issues by empirical methods. For the most part, positions on these issues depend on a person's philosophical outlook or preferred social theories. They can generate endless debate until other issues excite more interest. (The mind-body controversy was a metaphysical issue concerning the relation of mental processes to the brain and nerve structure of the body. The controversy was never settled, it just died down for many years — at least as far as psychologists were concerned — but might still reappear.)

In matters of social-philosophical theory we all have our preferences or personal tastes. *De gustibus non est disputandum* means that tastes should not be argued about. Our value judgments are tastes. I could never prove, empirically, that my value system was better than yours. Utilitarians, believing in the principle of the greatest happiness of the greatest number, might declare that ping-pong was better than poetry if more people enjoyed playing ping-pong; and similarly that the Beatles were better than Bach. Surveys might settle both questions of popularity but the basic principle (regarding the greatest happiness, and so on) remains untestable and therefore unresolved.

Value judgments are involved in many of the attacks that have been made against social surveys, especially those that have been made by radical sociologists whether or not they are Marxists. Close to this group and sometimes part of it are those humanists who believe that we need to look at people in a more subjective way, a way that is person-centred rather than research-centred; later I will attempt to explain their views about social surveys. These and other critics have said that social surveys are too passive; they would prefer to see more direct public participation in social planning. The opposing view regards surveys as too activating, changing the attitudes which are studied, and even arousing attitudes that people had not previously developed.

Some critics see surveys, especially public opinion polls, as a threat to democratic government; this is countered by the claim that democracy is strengthened through knowledge of public opinion. More specific in its attack is the claim that social surveys put too much stress on statistical significance at the expense of social significance or practical relevance.

I think all these views are important and can teach us to keep our methods under constant review. Though I am obviously biased, since I have written a book that I hope will encourage the use of social surveys, I will try to present these issues as fairly as possible. For the sake of clarity, over-simplification may be inevitable, which may be unjust in some cases. The remedy is to follow up these issues by further reading.

Some humanist issues may look at first like arguments about techniques; deeper inspection brings out value judgments. Some objections made against social surveys are based on criticisms regarding the use of closed questions. It is argued that fixed-choice questions restrict the range of possible responses so that respondents are not able to give a true picture of their thoughts. In many cases this is a serious limitation of the method and attempts should be made to remedy this defect. For example, preliminary fieldwork should broaden the investigator's understanding of the issues involved and the possible range of answers. Using an informal style of inquiry at this stage, a perceptive and receptive observer should be able to avoid framing questions that will exclude important information. In interviews, especially probes, he can draw out supplementary or qualifying statements; the inclusion of a few open questions can give more scope to the respondent.

To some extent we are really faced here with the choice of doing an intensive study of a few people or getting a more general picture based on a wider sample. In a social survey we may have to accept a method that would not be suitable for the clinical diagnosis of an individual. This hurts the humanist psychologists and the radical sociologists who believe that we should treat each person as the appropriate universe and accord each one as much importance as we give ourselves. This is fine and reflects a sincere devotion to the rights and characteristics of the respondent as a person. But the results of a survey can still be valid providing most people have found it possible to answer the important items to their satisfaction even in the restricted manner permitted.

A more fundamental objection is that even the prior selection of questions reflects our ideas about the survey population. For example, in drafting a set of questions for old people, my students included an item such as 'How often do friends visit you?' and did not ask how often the old people were able to visit their friends. Here again adequate preliminary work, giving people ample opportunity to speak for themselves and describe their daily lives, should prevent the formation of a restricted range of possibilities.

In the absence of any clear but restricted idea of what people are like, or perhaps what we would hope them to be like, we may expect them to resemble us. When the item 'Are you interested in politics?' was included in a draft interview form, my student interviewers predicted that respondents would ask for elaboration of this item; does 'politics' refer to Federal, State, or local politics? does 'interested' refer to reading about politics or taking an active part? These were reasonable comments but in trial runs only a few people asked for further explanation and these were mostly students of politics. The question was retained, with a standard elaboration if required, and proved to be useful. Perhaps the critics who object to fixed-choice questions are projecting their own dilemmas and so they exaggerate the subtlety of thought of most respondents. Roiser takes his own experience in answering a questionnaire as the starting point for a provocative essay on 'Asking Silly Questions'. However he also cites other examples from questionnaires[1] and I am not defending the kind of ambiguity and in-built bias that he criticises. With complex issues it is difficult to find out exactly what people think. Giving them sufficient space to write in their comments and 'what they find wrong' with the questions (as Roiser suggests) is one solution; using interviews with plenty of open questions and follow-up probes would be another.

A more sweeping criticism of social surveys could be based on Marxism, or at least on Bogart's interpretation of Marxism[3]. (see p. 147). According to this view, public opinion does not exist; there are different publics, or classes, with different ideologies. Since most social surveys use social class as a variable in order to compare the opinions of people from different sections of the population or from different levels of the class hierarchy, we can hardly disagree with the concept of different class ideologies. But some Marxists might go further and say, first, that the opinions of unenlightened un-class-conscious workers would only represent the false ideology instilled into them by their capitalist masters; and, second, that the ideology, the one that is in their own economic interest, is the only one which matters and this is in the safe hands of their class-conscious revolutionary leaders. On this view a survey is not only unnecessary, it would be misleading.

'THERE IS NO PLACE FOR PUBLIC OPINION'
True or False? Or don't you know?

There is no place for public opinion in the political theory of Marxism-Leninism, because the concept of 'the public' implies a single body politic, whether or not it is considered to be composed of uniform and homogeneous individual components — as implied in the philosophy of one man-one vote. As long as one puts emphasis on the separate publics represented by social classes, to each of which an appropriate political ideology corresponds, the significant clash of opinion must be that of the publics themselves, of their powers and essential interests, which opinions serve only to rationalize. Opinions that deviate from those appropriate to one's class are irrational; those unrelated to class interest are irrelevant. Thus, half a century after the October Revolution, there is still in the Soviet Union only the most primitive and reluctant acceptance of the notion that survey techniques may be usefully applied to the study of serious matters.[2]

The first point, regarding the nature and source of workers' opinions, is an empirical question. The evidence is mixed. Workers in many countries, and particularly in the USA, often agree with statements supporting private enterprise. Their criticisms of their conditions of employment may reflect dissatisfaction with the rewards that they receive for their work, without necessarily attacking their employers as representatives of the capitalist system. But there is never any certainty, except perhaps in authoritarian régimes, that every section of public opinion will exactly represent the official dogma of the establishment. Social planners might still like to know what the workers think, even though to some social theorists it seems obvious that what the workers think is unrealistic.

The second point, which claims to distinguish a true ideology from a false one, is a value judgment. This can be argued on the basis of social theory, but of course it cannot be settled by measuring opinions and attitudes. On these grounds Marxists are right in dismissing surveys as irrelevant. Opinion polls can neither validate nor invalidate value judgments; no social scientist has ever claimed that they could.

Others besides Marxists have claimed that surveys are unnecessary and misleading. On several occasions trade-union representatives have told me that there was no need for me to interview their members; they claimed that through branch meetings and personal contact they had a clear picture of the workers' attitudes; factory managers have made similar claims. In most cases they have accepted my argument that some people are different and these differences are often interesting, and therefore I need first-hand contact. Some managers have still objected on the grounds that my questions might 'put ideas into their heads'. Perhaps without realising it these union officials and managers are acting on the basis of a socio-political theory that Roiser says is 'conservative and constitutional. It admits only of gradual change from recognised differences of viewpoint.'

Roiser argues that as a consequence of accepting this theory 'which maintains that there is only a single valid consensus of meaning within a given society', social scientists may construct a rigid framework and a single attitude scale; consequently 'deviant perspectives are denied'.[4]

The importance of letting people speak for themselves, and not constructing a rigid framework as the basis for asking questions in a survey, is emphasised by social phenomenologists. They appeal for the study of phenomena (in this case, people's thoughts and feelings) as they are, without the intervention of preconceived concepts and analytical systems. Phenomenologists (and many others) express strong dissatisfaction with the statistical orientation of surveys and the sweeping generalisations that leave people out of account. These criticisms are aimed at 'the more structured methods such as questionnaires [which] tend to define and limit the expression of experience by the use of predefined categories'[5]. The importance of informal, open preliminary exploration or good qualitative pilot work is recognised with some reservations; there is usually a plea for good interviewing, or 'proper' interviewing[6] with discussions and open questions. However, open questions have to be coded and this could lead back into a restrictive framework.

Another form of criticism, which also doubts the value of question-naires, comes from what is now known as 'ethnomethodology'. One basic proposition of ethnomethodology is that people should be studied naturalistically. This has always been stressed by anthropologists and the principle applies just as much to people within our own culture. Standing on the door-step, answering questions put by a stranger, is not a natural activity, nor is filling in a questionnaire. Some interviews, if they are conducted like ordinary conversations, and some discussions in small groups, can be quite natural. Combined with participant observation, these methods probably bring us as close to another person's inner experience as we can ever hope to be. Psychoanalysis has shown how difficult it is for one person to look into the inner experience of another. Too often we may rely on what a person chooses to tell us about private thoughts and feelings; we sense a person's inner experience through that person's descriptions and accounts of events in the outside world; in the end we are forced back upon *our* interpretations. This is the best that we can do in most surveys and we may need to check our interpretations against other data. Do the same people who deplore violence also watch boxing on television?

There are two other criticisms of social surveys that seem to contradict each other. The first says that social surveys can create attitudes that did not exist; this would be the belief of those factory managers who feared that my surveys might put ideas into the heads of their workers. The second criticism regards surveys as too passive for the people who are questioned; they may learn nothing, and even if they do, any application of the conclusions of the survey is not in their hands. Perhaps social surveys are both active (first criticism) *and* passive (second criticism): though as generalisations they appear to conflict, it is possible that for some surveys and for some individuals one or both might be valid. Let us examine each in detail.

Surveys often include questions that assume that the respondent has already formed an opinion on the topic or holds a relevant attitude that enables an answer to be made. There are ways of checking this assumption. But the point is that whether the respondent had thought about the matter before or not, being asked questions could easily stimulate a new interest. Subsequently the matter might be discussed in conversations with friends or neighbours; newspaper items might be noticed which previously would have passed unnoticed. These consequences are not necessarily bad but as a result of answering questions in a survey people might become dissatisfied with things which they previously accepted; the factory workers might begin to think that their factory was an unhealthy place to work in. Another consequence of taking part in a survey is that people might expect that something would be done about their complaints or suggestions. This is not an unreasonable expectation especially if their co-operation had been obtained following a hint of the possibility of some benefit to the community. There may be good reasons for not being able to please everybody; some suggestions may cancel out, as when one group wants a bowling green while another group wants a child care centre on the same piece of land. Cost, legal difficulties and practical considerations may prevent some popular requests. In the end, according to this criticism, people are more frustrated than they were before.

Social scientists who think that there is a need for the community to become aware of their social environment and become more involved in social action, are unlikely to be worried by this type of criticism. In fact they are more likely to make the opposite claim, that social surveys are too passive. There is obviously some truth in this. Respondents do not usually have any choice in the questions they are asked in the survey nor do they see the results. Some surveys overcome this. During the preliminary pilot work interested groups are invited to suggest questions and in exploratory interviews people are asked for their suggestions; summary reports may be published in the local press or presented at meetings of interested groups and the full reports may be made available to all who apply. The complaint is that this procedure is exceptional whereas it should be normal practice.

Even this would not be enough in many cases. The Skeffington Report urges the need for public participation through meetings and exhibitions as well as through representation on committees; the report proposes that this participation should proceed in parallel with a series of social surveys and that there should be cross-fertilisation at every stage. Survey results would be discussed at public meetings; public discussion should generate questions for the next survey.

One survey organisation director sees a danger in taking too much notice of the active minority that attends public meetings. Leonard England believes that the Skeffington procedure 'gives every opportunity for any pressure groups to make themselves felt'. As a consequence, he says, public consultation over planning must always aid only the opposition to any planning proposal. He claims that professionally conducted objective public opinion surveys, using random samples, are needed to ascertain the views of the population of the area as a whole.[7]

Contrary to Leonard England's view, the opposition does not always gain support through public participation. In May 1974 an Australian survey in the Albury-Wodonga district found that 64 per cent were against 'accelerated' growth in that area; people in streets and shops were approached on a random basis and interviewed; the sample of 820 was about 2 per cent of the population.[8] In June and July the Development Corporation held an exhibition displaying alternative growth proposals, which is one form of public participation advocated by the Skeffington report. Visitors to the exhibition were invited to complete questionnaires and about one in five did so; the resulting sample of 1500 was 3.6 per cent of the population. In sharp contrast to the street survey, a majority of the visitors (65 per cent) *favoured* 'the selection of Albury-Wodonga as a growth centre'.[9] Though the word 'accelerated' was not used, the display maps were intended to carry the same idea. Other differences in survey methods could also account for some of the apparent swing in public opinion, but the Albury-Wodonga Development Corporation believed that the results showed a 'majority acceptance of the planning proposals once details had been made public'.[10]

It was suggested earlier that some critics claim that social surveys in general and public opinion polls in particular are a threat to the democratic processes of government. Three points can be made to support this claim; they relate to the possible effects of surveys on elections, on politicians, and on parliamentary discussion and supremacy.

We do not know for certain what are the effects of publishing election forecasts that are usually based on public opinion polls. Sometimes a candidate or party may benefit from the bandwagon effect, that is, marginal voters may decide to support the most likely winner. On the other hand the publication of forecasts showing a safe majority may actually hinder the leading party in two ways. First, the party's supporters may slacken their campaign efforts; and second, especially when voting is not compulsory, apathy and failure to vote may damage the side which looks certain to win. This apathy could also affect their opponents, but perhaps not to the same extent. If in addition there is a sympathy vote for the obvious loser, the predicted safe majority might disappear. Some of these factors, together with others (such as the weather) might help to explain the result of the British election in 1970; nearly all forecasts put Labour well ahead, but on polling day they were defeated by the Conservatives. Another possible effect of publishing election forecasts is that the smaller minority parties may find it difficult to attract supporters if opinion polls repeatedly show that they do not have a chance of winning.

We can only guess how politicians might be swayed by surveys; perhaps it is possible that some of them might be influenced against their own better judgment. This assumes, of course, that politicians are wiser than the people they represent; perhaps they are. The politicians certainly think so and make decisions about the death penalty, the adoption of the metric system, space exploration, building nuclear weapons, and joining in a war (just to quote a few actual examples) without putting these items in their election policies or submitting them, in any systematic way, to public opinion.

Whether parliamentary discussion would suffer as the result of a greater use of social surveys is debatable. It would certainly be difficult for a Member to urge one policy and claim to speak for the people after a public opinion poll had just shown that the majority favoured a different policy. Critics of social surveys could argue that Parliament is the proper place for informed discussion and important matters of policy cannot be decided by door-step interviews however extensive and systematic.

In Australia the Constitution specifies that certain matters shall be decided by a referendum of the whole electorate. We now know that a 5 per cent probability sample would cost less and be just as valid; but there are good reasons for not adopting a sampling procedure. People would complain that they were not consulted, just as people often question the validity of public opinion polls on the grounds that they have never been interviewed. A sample referendum is unlikely to produce extensive public discussion. People are less likely to think about the issue and be ready for information on the off-chance that they may be included in the sample. A referendum that is part of the decision-making machinery is quite different from a social survey that could be part of the information service on which decisions may be based.

As presented here, none of these threats to democracy appear to be very substantial. The reader will make allowances for any obvious bias in the discussion. Counter-claims, that social surveys assist the democratic process, will be stated very briefly.

First, it is possible that public opinion polls actually stimulate interest in elections. The fluctuations reported in the press, the continual counting of heads, remind people that they have a voice and must soon make a decision. On the second point it could be said that politicians should take more notice of public opinion when it is systematically assessed, and not rely on party or newspaper guesses. The purpose of being accurately informed about public opinion is not merely to ensure capturing votes; policy discussions should give some weight to the state of public readiness for changes. Social surveys can reveal how opinion is related to other factors and whether more information is required about current or forthcoming issues.

Finally, on the third point, social surveys should be used as part of the participatory process and not as a substitute for decision making. The way social planning could be improved through a continuous process that combines and interrelates social surveys with public discussion and committee work is described graphically in the Skeffington Report.

There may be other controversial issues. Social scientists are in a turmoil regarding their function in society. Most of them appear to believe that they can increase human happiness within the framework of the existing social order. The changes that they sometimes facilitate are directed towards the more efficient use of human and other resources. Others believe they should be active rather than passive change agents, suggesting, urging, implementing alternative social patterns, not merely acting as servants of the established order. To take a neutral position in this controversy is to be accused of serving the interests of the existing system at the expense of reform or radical change; or else to be accused of failing to use the system in the interest of constructive change.

We should be aware of these controversial issues and the others in this chapter without being incapacitated by them. Carrying out social surveys is one way of learning about other people and of discovering for ourselves the strengths and weaknesses of survey methods. Admittedly some practitioners may become addicted as a result of enjoying the survey experience, and shield themselves from any controversial aspects. Others will find that their understanding of the human condition becomes more sympathetic and their appreciation of the controversial aspects becomes sharper and based on experience rather than prejudice.

Finally, I suggest that the following principles should be adopted as guidelines. In order to avoid the use of social surveys for exploitation rather than exploration, we should be able to answer 'Yes' to the following questions:

1. Can I honestly say that the survey is in the interests of the survey population, or at least is not against their interests?

2. Am I prepared to share my information with them, say in a tabulated form (to preserve anonymity)?

3. Will I make it possible for the people involved (or their representatives) to discuss the results with me?

Any social tool can be used for good or evil. The responsibility is yours.

Notes

[1] pp. 101-14 in Armistead, *op. cit.*

[2] From L. Bogart, 'No opinion, Don't know and maybe no answer', *Public Opinion Quarterly,* vol. 31, 1967, pp. 331-45.

[3] *ibid.*

[4] Armistead, *op. cit.,* p. 112.

[5] *ibid.,* p. 119.

[6] A.V. Cicourel, *Method and measurement in sociology,* Free Press of Glencoe, New York, 1964, pp. 85-6.

[7] *New Society,* 9 May 1974, pp. 315-16.

[8] Wodonga Technical School Report, October 1974 (mimeo).

[9] Albury-Wodonga Development Corporation, *Analysis of exhibition questionnaire,* September 1974 (mimeo).

[10] Personal communication, Albury-Wodonga Development Corporation, 4 February 1975.

Further reading

Recent developments in humanistic psychology, phenomenology, and related ideas are discussed in a collection of essays (Armistead (ed.), 1974). The sections most relevant to the issues raised in this chapter are: Martin Roiser, 'Asking silly questions', (pp. 101-14); Nigel Armistead, 'Experience in everyday life', (pp. 115-32); and David Triesman, 'The radical use of official data', (pp. 295-313).

Cicourel, 1964, discusses the problems involved in the use of fixed-choice questions in his ch. 4. The book raises many other issues relating to social research methods. Cicourel is now regarded as one of the leading exponents of social phenomenology.

Finally, here is a reminder about the standard textbooks that will take you further into many of the problems I have discussed in this book: Goode & Hatt, 1952; Moser & Kalton, 1971; Selltiz *et al.*, 1960; and Young, 1966.

Appendix A
Interpreting Correlations

A correlation between two factors, A and B, which is not a spurious or nonsense correlation[1] may be the result of interaction between them. By itself, a correlation coefficient only expresses a mathematical or statistical relationship indicating that to the extent that one variable is present, the other is either present (positive coefficient) or absent (negative coefficient). But our scientific curiosity takes us further than this and we wonder why two factors should be statistically related in this way. In other words we hope to explain a statistical relationship (a correlation) in terms of a causal relationship or model. Perhaps one factor 'causes' or determines the other; this gives us two possibilities: either A is the cause and B the effect, or B is the cause and A the effect. Another possibility is that the interaction is circular, each factor affecting the other. If sufficient is known about the antecedent conditions, a fourth possibility might be tested, namely, that both factors are effects of a common cause; A and B increase or decrease together, or as one increases the other decreases, not because they directly affect each other but because a common factor X affects them both.

Ideally these speculations should be based upon some general theory and then submitted to the test by some appropriately designed survey or experiment. But a moment's reflection will show that the possible explanations can be combined in numerous ways, so numerous that they cannot be tested by a single investigation.

Let us suppose that between two factors, A and B, there may be

  (a) no direct causal relationship ('non-causal')
  (b) a causal relationship from A to B
  (c) a causal relationship from B to A
  (d) a circular causal interaction.

This gives us three independent forms of linkage and a fourth that is the combination of the second and third. The first is 'non-causal' and the rest 'causal'.

Now let us suppose that there may or may not be a common cause 'X'; or X may be a mediating factor between A and B (for example, A affects X which affects B so that A is the indirect 'cause' of B via X), or X may even be a common effect of both A and B. Again there are the four possible links between X and A and between X and B. These possibilities may be combined: three factors with four different kinds of connection between each pair, thus:

pair	links
X & A	(a) (b) (c) (d)
X & B	(a) (b) (c) (d)
A & B	(a) (b) (c) (d)

making in all a total of 4 × 4 × 4 theoretical possibilities, or 64.

When a significant correlation is found between A and B, how many of these possibilities can be eliminated? We can rule out the case with three non-causal links:

$$X$$
$$(a) \quad (a)$$
$$A \ (a) \ B$$

These triads can be represented on one line, thus:

$$X \quad (a) \quad A \quad (a) \quad B \quad (a) \quad X \tag{1}$$

Moreover, if A and B are statistically related, then there must be something more than a non-causal link between X and A and between A and B, whatever the connection between X and B. So we can rule out

$$X \quad (a) \quad A \quad (a) \quad B \quad (b) \quad X \tag{2}$$
$$X \quad (a) \quad A \quad (a) \quad B \quad (c) \quad X \tag{3}$$
$$X \quad (a) \quad A \quad (a) \quad B \quad (d) \quad X \tag{4}$$

In other words, however X and B may be connected, such connection by itself could not explain a correlation between A and B. Similarly, as regards X and A, non-causal links between X and A and between A and B are insufficient to explain a statistical relationship between A and B. This rules out

$$X \quad (b) \quad A \quad (a) \quad B \quad (a) \quad X \tag{5}$$
$$X \quad (c) \quad A \quad (a) \quad B \quad (a) \quad X \tag{6}$$
$$X \quad (d) \quad A \quad (a) \quad B \quad (a) \quad X \tag{7}$$

So far our 64 varieties have been reduced to 57.

Now if X is the common *effect* of A and B, then the link between A and B must either be directly causal or indirectly causal via X. So out goes

$$X \quad (c) \quad A \quad (a) \quad B \quad (b) \quad X \tag{8}$$

This leaves us with a total of 56 possibilities.

The various possibilities are listed in Table 1. It will be seen that when there is a one-way or a two-way causal connection between A and B, (b), (c) or (d), then in each case all four possibilities may exist between X and A, X and B, i.e., 3 × 4 × 4 making 48. The more complicated situation is when no direct causal link exists between A and B (when a correlation is nevertheless found between them), in which case either X must be a common cause (four) or X must be the indirect link between A and B (another four) — total 56.

TABLE 1
Possible Causal Explanations or Models given a Significant Correlation, A & B with X as a Possible Common Factor

Key
No direct causal link = (a)
Direct causal link   = (b)
Reverse causal link   = (c)
Circular causal link   = (d)

TYPE 1 — A causes B, *link (b):*
    may occur with —
X & A   (a) (b) (c) (d) ⎤
X & B   (a) (b) (c) (d) ⎦   4 × 4   16

TYPE 2 — B causes A, *link (c):*
    may occur with —
X & A   (a) (b) (c) (d) ⎤
X & B   (a) (b) (c) (d) ⎦   4 × 4   16

TYPE 3 — A & B *Circular, link (d):*
    may occur with —
X & A   (a) (b) (c) (d) ⎤
X & B   (a) (b) (c) (d) ⎦   4 × 4   16
                                                    —
                                                  48

TYPE 4 — A & B, *no direct causal link (a):*
    with X *common cause*
X & A   (b) or (d) ⎤
A & B   (b) or (d) ⎦   2 × 2   4

TYPE 5 — A & B *indirectly linked*
    through X; A & B = (a):
X & A   (b) or (d) ⎤
X & B   (c)   ⎦   2 × 1   2
X & A   (c)   ⎤
X & B   (b) or (d) ⎦   2 × 1   2
                                     Total   56

This shows that a correlation between two variables may be explained in 56 different ways. In some cases the known temporal relations eliminate some of the possibilities. Even so, adequate systematic investigation is necessary before one is justified in selecting what are considered to be the most likely explanations. The complexity of the problem can be seen in the examples given in the section on 'Explanatory Interpretation' in Chapter 9.

Finally, a reminder. As explained in that section, the concept of causal explanation or causal model must not be taken too literally.[2]

Notes

[1]G.W. Snedecor & William G. Cochran, *Statistical methods,* 6th edn, Iowa State University Press, 1967, p. 189.

[2]F.N. Kerlinger & E.J. Pedhazur, *Multiple regression in behavioral research,* Holt, Rinehart & Winston, New York, 1973, p. 306.

References

Abrams, M. *Social surveys and social action.* Heinemann, London, 1951.
Argyle, M., Gardner, G. & Ciffi, F. 'The measurement of supervisory methods'. *Human Relations,* vol. 10, 1957, pp. 295–313.
Argyle, M. *The social psychology of work.* Penguin, Harmondsworth, 1974.
Armistead, M. (ed.) *Reconstructing social psychology,* Penguin, Harmondsworth, 1974.
Atkinson, J. *A handbook for interviewers: a manual for Government Social Survey interviewing staff, describing practice and procedures on structured interviewing.* HMSO, London, 1967.
Bartholomew, D.J. & Bassett, E.E. *Let's look at the figures: the quantitative approach to human affairs.* Penguin, Harmondsworth, 1971.
Barzun, J. & Graff, H.F. *The modern researcher.* rev. edn. Harcourt, Brace & World, New York, 1970.
Belson, W.A. 'The effects of reversing the presentation order of verbal rating scales'. *Journal of Advertising Research,* vol. 6, no. 4, 1966. Reprint Series No. 37.
––––––– 'Respondent understanding of survey questions'. *Polls,* vol. 4, no. 3, 1968. Reprint Series No. 40.
Belson, W.A. & Duncan, J.A. 'A comparison of the check list and the open response questioning systems'. *Applied Statistics,* vol. 11, 1962, pp. 120–32. Reprint Series No. 29.
Blalock Jr, H.M. *Causal inferences in non-experimental research.* University of North Carolina Press, Chapel Hill, N.C., 1964.
Blalock Jr, H.M. & Blalock, A.B. (eds) *Methodology in social research.* McGraw-Hill, New York, 1968, ch. 8.
Bogart, L. 'No opinion, don't know, and maybe no answer'. *Public Opinion Quarterly,* vol. 31, 1967, pp. 331–45.
Booth, C. (ed.) *Labour and the life of the people of London.* 17 vols, Macmillan, London, 1889–1902.
Buzzard, R.B. 'Notes on report writing'. *Occupational Psychology,* vol. 46, 1972, pp. 201–7.
Cantril, H. (ed.) *Gauging public opinion.* Princeton University Press, Princeton, N.J., 1944.
Cicourel, A.V. *Method and measurement in sociology.* Free Press of Glencoe, New York, 1964.
Cochran, G. Sampling techniques. 2nd edn. Wiley, New York, 1966.
Collins, W.A. 'Interviewers' verbal idiosyncracies as a source of bias'. *Public Opinion Quarterly,* vol. 34, 1970, pp. 416–22.
Congalton, A.A. *Status and prestige in Australia.* Cheshire, Melbourne, 1969.
Dandenong Ranges Report. The Victorian Public Interest Research Group Ltd, Monash University, 1974.
Davies, A.F. & Encel, S. *Australian society.* 2nd edn. Cheshire, Melbourne, 1970.
Denzin, N.K. *Sociological methods: a sourcebook.* Butterworth, London, 1970.
Dohrenwend, B.S. 'An experimental study of directive interviewing'. *Public Opinion Quarterly,* vol. 34, 1970, pp. 117–25.
Durbin, J. 'Non-response and call-backs in surveys'. *Bulletin of the International Statistical Institute,* vol. 34, no. 2, 1954, pp. 72–86.
Durbin, J. & Stuart, A. 'Callbacks and clustering in sample surveys: an experimental study'. *Journal of the Royal Statistical Society,* Series A, vol. 117, no. 4, 1954, pp. 387–428.
Emery, F.E. & Oeser, O.A. *Information, decision and action.* Melbourne University Press. 1958.

Festinger, L. & Katz, D. (eds) *Research methods in the behavioural sciences.* The Dryden Press, New York, 1953.

Festinger, L., Riecken, J. & Schachter, S. *When prophecy fails.* University of Minnesota Press, Minneapolis, 1956.

Gans, H.J. *The urban villagers: group and class in the life of Italian-Americans.* Free Press, New York, 1962.

———— *The Levittowners: ways of life and politics in a new suburban community.* Pantheon Books, New York, 1967.

Gardner, G., Sheil, B.A. & Taylor, V.A. 'Passive politics: a survey of Melbourne University students'. *Politics,* vol. V, no. 1, May 1970, pp. 30–7.

Gardner, G. *Student demonstrators at Melbourne University.* Paper presented at the sixth Annual Conference of the Australian Psychological Society, August 1971.

Gombrich, E.H. *Art and illusion.* new edn. Phaidon, London, 1962.

———— *The story of art.* 8th edn. Phaidon, London, 1957.

Goodchild, B. 'Class differences in environmental perception: an exploratory study'. *Urban Studies,* vol. 11, 1974, pp. 157–69.

Goode, W.J. & Hatt, P.K. *Methods in social research.* McGraw-Hill, New York, 1952.

Gowers, E. (revised by Sir Bruce Fraser) *The complete plain words.* Penguin, Harmondsworth, 1974.

Gray, P.G. 'A sample survey with both a postal and an interview stage'. *Applied Statistics,* vol. 6, 1957, pp. 139–53.

Hammond, S.B. *Boy and man.* Department of Psychology, University of Melbourne, 1974, mimeo.

Hansen, M.H., Hurwitz, W.N. & Madow, W.G. *Sample survey methods and theory, Vol. 1: Methods and applications.* Wiley, New York, 1953.

Hauck, M. 'Is survey postcard verification effective?'. *Public Opinion Quarterly,* vol. 33, 1969, pp. 117–20.

Henderson, R.F., Harcourt, A. & Harper, R.J.A. *People in poverty: a Melbourne survey.* Cheshire, for the Institute of Applied Economic and Social Research, University of Melbourne, 1970.

Horder, Lord. 'The General Practitioner and lay education in cancer'. Letter to the Editor, *Lancet,* vol. 2, 1953, p. 137.

Hughes, A. *Psychology and the political experience.* Cambridge University Press, 1975.

Hyman, H.H., Cobb, W.J., Hart, C.W. & Stember, C.H. *Interviewing in social research.* University of Chicago Press, 1954.

Hyman, H. *Survey design and analysis: principles, cases and procedures.* Free Press, Glencoe, Ill., 1955.

Jones, F.L. *Dimensions of urban social structure.* ANU Press, Canberra, 1969.

———— 'A social ranking of Melbourne suburbs'. *Australian and New Zealand Journal of Sociology,* vol. 3, October 1967, pp. 93–110.

Kahn, R.L. & Cannell, C.F. *The dynamics of interviewing: theory, technique and cases.* Wiley, New York, 1957.

Kerlinger, F.N. & Pedhazur, E.J. *Multiple regression in behavioral research.* Holt, Rinehart & Winston, New York, 1973.

Kinsey, A.C., Pomeroy, W.B. & Martin, C.E. *Sexual behavior in the human male.* Saunders, Philadelphia, 1948.

————, ———— & ————. *Sexual behavior in the human female.* Saunders, Philadelphia, 1953.

Kish, L. Survey sampling. Wiley, New York, 1965.

Lazarsfeld, P.F. & Rosenberg, M. *The language of social research.* Free Press, Glencoe, Ill., 1955.

Lindzey, G. (ed.) *Handbook of social psychology.* Addison-Wesley, Cambridge, Mass., 1954.

Lindzey, G. & Aronson, E. (eds) *The handbook of social psychology.* 2nd edn. Addison-Wesley, Reading, 'Mass., 1968.

Lumsden, J. *Elementary statistical method.* University of Western Australia Press, Nedlands, 1969.

Lyons, R. *Patient attitudes toward the Preston and Northcote Community Hospital.* MSc thesis in Occupational Psychology, University of Melbourne, 1974.

Mann, L. 'Attitudes towards My Lai and obedience to orders: an Australian survey'. *Australian Journal of Psychology,* vol. 25, no. 1, 1973, pp. 11–21.

Mogey, J.M. *Family and neighbourhood.* Oxford University Press, 1956.

Morris, T. *The criminal area.* Routledge and Kegan Paul, London, 1957.

Moser, C.A. *Survey methods in social investigation.* Heinemann, London, 1958.

Moser, C.A. & Kalton, G. *Survey methods in social investigation.* 2nd edn. Heinemann, London, 1971.

Oeser, O.A. & Emery, F.E. *Social structure and personality in a rural community.* Routledge and Kegan Paul, London, 1954.

Oppenheim, A.N. *Questionnaire design and attitude measurement.* Basic Books, New York, 1966.
Pahl, R.E. *Readings in urban sociology.* Pergamon Press, Oxford, 1968.
Parkin, F. *Middle class radicalism: the social bases of the British campaign for nuclear disarmament.* Melbourne University Press, 1968.
Payne, S.L.B. *The art of asking questions.* Princeton University Press, 1951.
Reiss Jr, A.J. *Occupations and social status.* Free Press, New York, 1961.
Robb, J.H. *Working-class anti-Semite: a psychological study in a London borough.* Tavistock Publications, London, 1954.
Roethlisberger, F.J. and Dickson, W.J. *Management and the worker: an account of a research program conducted by the Western Electric Company, Hawthorne Works, Chicago.* Harvard University Press, Cambridge, Mass., 1939.
Rogers, C.R. 'The nondirective method as a technique for social research'. *American Journal of Sociology,* vol. 50, 1945, pp. 279–83.
Rowntree, B.S. *Poverty: a study of town life.* 2nd edn. Macmillan, London, 1902.
_____ *Poverty and progress: a second social survey of York.* Longmans Green, London, 1941.
Russell, B. *An outline of philosophy.* Allen & Unwin, London, 1927.
Schofield, M. *Sociological aspects of homosexuality: a comparative study of three types of homosexuals.* Longmans, London, 1965.
_____ *The sexual behavior of young people.* Longmans, London. rev. edn. Penguin, Harmondsworth, 1968.
_____. *Social research.* Heinemann, (Concept Books, No. 8), London, 1969.
_____. *The strange case of pot.* Penguin, Harmondsworth, 1971.
Schuman, H. & Converse, J.M. 'The effects of black and white interviewers on black responses in 1968'. *Public Opinion Quarterly,* vol. 35, 1971, pp. 44–68.
Scott, C. 'Research on mail surveys'. *Journal of the Royal Statistical Society,* A, vol. 124, 1961, pp. 143–205.
Scott, W.H. *Industrial leadership and joint consultation.* University of Liverpool Press, 1952, Appendix B.
Selltiz, C., Jahoda, M., Deutsch, M. & Cook, S.W. *Research methods in social relations.* rev. edn. Holt-Dryden, New York, 1960.
Shapiro, M.J. 'Discovering interviewer bias in open-ended survey responses'. *Public Opinion Quarterly,* vol. 34, 1970, pp. 412–15.
Skeffington, A.M. *People and planning.* Report of the Committee on Public Participation and Planning, HMSO, London, 1969.
Smeiser, N.J. & Smelser, W.T. (eds) *Personality and social systems.* Wiley, New York, 1963.
Snedecor, G.W. *Statistical methods.* 4th edn. Iowa State College Press, 1946.
Stacey, M. *Tradition and change: a study of Banbury.* Oxford University Press, 1960.
_____ *Methods of social research.* Pergamon Press, Oxford, 1969.
Stanley, G., Boots, M. & Johnson, C. 'Some Australian data on the short version of the Attitudes to Women Scale (AWS)'. *Australian Psychologist,* vol. 10, no. 2, 1975.
Stevenson, A., Martin, E., & O'Neill, J. *High living: a study of family life in flats.* Melbourne University Press, 1967.
Stouffer, S.A., Guttman, L.A., Schuman, E.A., Lazarsfeld, P.F., Star, S.A. & Clausen, J.A. *Studies in social psychology in World War II, Vol. IV, Measurement and prediction.* Princeton University Press, 1950.
Stretton, H. *Ideas for Australian cities.* Georgian House, Melbourne, 1973.
Sudman, S. *Reducing the cost of surveys.* Aldine Publishing Co., Chicago, 1967.
Survey Research Center, University of Michigan. *Interviewers' manual.* Institute for Social Research, University of Michigan, Ann Arbor, Mich., 1969.
Tull, D.S. & Albaum, G.S. *Survey research: a decisional approach.* International Textbooks, Aylesbury, UK, 1973.
Vaughan, E.J. *Perception of work among factory workers.* MA thesis, University of Melbourne, 1974.
Whyte, W.F. *Street corner society: the social structure of an Italian slum.* 2nd edn. University of Chicago Press, 1955.
Willmott, P. *The evolution of a community.* Routledge & Kegan Paul, London, 1963.
Willmott, P. & Young, M. *Family and class in a London suburb.* Routledge & Kegan Paul, London, 1960.
Yates, F. *Sampling methods for censuses and surveys.* 3rd edn. Hafner, New York, 1960.
Young, M. & Willmott, P. *Family and kinship in East London.* Routledge & Kegan Paul, London, 1957.
Young, P.V. *Scientific social surveys and research: an introduction to the background, content, methods, principles, and analysis of social studies.* 4th edn. Prentice-Hall, Englewood Cliffs, N.J., 1966.
Zweig, F. *Labour, life and poverty.* Gollancz, London, 1948.

Name Index

Subject Index